Retail fans can now take strolls down memory lane with Lisicky, a department store historian.
—Boston Globe

You might think of Michael Lisicky's obsession with department stores as an orchestral tone poem for a single oboe: at turns plaintive and raucous, eloquent and funny, with unpredictable little swerves.
—Baltimore Sun

Like veterans of a noble cause—a battle or an expedition—former employees of Woodward & Lothrop came forward to share their memories after the recent column on Lisicky's book. Customers did, too.
—Washington Post

If you're interested in department store history, buy his books.
—Philadelphia Inquirer

SHOP
POMEROY'S
FIRST

MICHAEL J. LISICKY

THE
History
PRESS

Published by The History Press
Charleston, SC 29403
www.historypress.net

Cover image of doorman from the collection of Lois Witmer.

First published 2014

Manufactured in the United States

ISBN 978.1.62619.565.3

Library of Congress CIP data applied for.

To Paul, Bobby and 333 North Second Street.

CONTENTS

Foreword, by Albert Boscov   9

Acknowledgements   13

Introduction   15

1. Placing a Keystone   17

2. Capital Gains   25

3. Greater Pomeroy's   37

4. Allied Forces   43

5. Pomeroy Days   51

6. Ever Changing, Ever Interesting   61

7. Around Town   69

8. 5/5/55   82

9. Beyond the City Limits   91

10. While Supplies Last   110

11. Bon Voyage   123

Appendix. Shopper's Special   143

Notes   147

Index   155

About the Author   159

FOREWORD

When I was growing up, there were three stores in downtown Reading, Pennsylvania. Pomeroy's was the largest, Whitner's was a little "higher up" and Read's catered to the lower end. Pomeroy's was the *real* department store, and it was the best department store at Christmastime. We went to Pomeroy's to visit Santa and received some free candy. Then we would go to Harold's Furniture to visit Santa and get free candy and then go to Kaufmann's to visit Santa and get free candy. You just went up and down Penn Street getting free candy. I was not really a shopper, and besides, I didn't have any money after visiting three Santa Clauses. I don't think we believed in Santa, but we did believe in candy; we had our own store but no Santa.

If Pomeroy's was the "big store," Boscov's was the neighborhood store. We were a little "pipsqueak." Our first store was located at Ninth and Pike Streets, and my dad expanded the store by buying the neighboring house and putting a hole through the wall. I grew up in the store. My first job was catching flies when I was six years old. I got a dime for every ten flies that I caught, which was the cost of seeing a movie at the Strand. That first week, I had a lot of trouble. The flies didn't want to be caught, so I would keep them, half of them, dead or alive. My father caught on, and instead I got a lecture on integrity.

My father was a lovely man, the sweetest guy in the world. I always enjoyed working in the store. It was a pleasant life. I was selling shoes by the time I was twelve. The store was just a part of our lives. Our sign said, "Economy Shoe

A cover of a 1960s-era employee manual depicts the classic American department store doorman. *Collection of Lois Witmer.*

and Dry Goods" on one side and "Boscov's Dept. Store" next to the other sign. We were a neighborhood store, but we had only about twenty thousand square feet. We knew that we couldn't compete with Pomeroy's, but over time, we ended up getting customers from more than just our neighborhood.

Downtown became a disaster after they tore down several big blocks to build a proposed shopping mall. These blocks were home to several smaller specialty stores. Downtown was no longer a draw. We saw what was going on in downtown Reading and decided to expand in the suburbs. If the mall was built, we'd reconsider. We ended up becoming the dominant store in Reading. By the 1980s, Pomeroy's was bringing in about $6 million a year in sales; we were bringing in about $36 million annually in sales.

Boscov's has a dedicated staff of people. We are in the market every week. We always keep working at being better. At this point, we can dominate a market. Retailing should be fun; it is recreation. I remember my father had a dream to have a store as big as Pomeroy's. Look at us now.

ALBERT BOSCOV
Chairman and Chief Executive Officer, Boscov's Department Stores

ACKNOWLEDGEMENTS

This book could not have been possible without the generous contributions from friends, family and former competitors of Pomeroy's Inc. The memories and comments of department store CEO Albert Boscov, through the assistance of Vivian Stephenson, helped personalize the story of Pomeroy's, Reading and Boscov's. Special gratitude is given to the Bon-Ton Stores Inc. and its chief executive officer, Tim Grumbacher, for sharing memories and allowing special access into the company archives, along with the assistance of Bon-Ton's Mary Kerr, Deb Copas and Mary Paumeri. Additional behind-the-scenes insight and historical knowledge was gratefully received from former Allied Stores executive Lee D. Starr. A big thank-you goes to Pomeroy family members Kathy Hayden, James Seivers and Barbara and David Korczykowski, all of whom provided special insights into the George Pomeroy family. Reading historian George M. Meiser IX was an invaluable and important resource bridging that city's past and present.

Numerous archival institutions provided wonderful services for this book's publication. Appreciation goes to Kimberly R. Brown and the staff at the Historical Society of Berks County Museum & Library, Barbara Breidenstein at the Pennsylvania History Room at the Reading Public Library, the staff at the *Reading Eagle*, Ken Frew and Nicole McMullen from the Historical Society of Dauphin County, the staff of the Dauphin County Library System's East Shore Area Library, the Pennsylvania State Archives, Dr. Peter Yasenchak and the staff at the Historical Society of Schuylkill County, librarian Jane Moyer at the Northampton County

Historical and Genealogical Society, Tiffany Lukashefski and Peggie Phillips at the Osterhout Free Library, Amanda Fontenova of the Luzerne County Historical Society, Thomas Mooney and Jon O'Connell of the *Wilkes-Barre Times Leader*, John Maday of the Greater Wilkes-Barre Chamber of Commerce and photographer John Rygiel.

Deep gratitude goes to the Pomeroy community who answered my phone calls and helped provide archival materials and memories. Lois Witmer and Leonard Miller generously donated many of the book's archival materials, while invaluable and informative conversations were had with Shirley Becker, June Bonning, Carol Brightbill, Mike Carratilo, Mary Custer, Pat Eichorn, Bettijane Long Eisenpreis, Bettie Hazzard, Anthony Kutchever, John Matusek, Dorothy Mugford, Ross Ricketts, John J. Rygiel, Margaret Shipula and the lively and ever-helpful Lee Spitalny. Additional memories were wonderfully collected from proud Pennsylvanians such as Norma Cresswell, Jean Dellock, Florence Ditlow, Dolores McKenna and John Whitner Rick.

I am grateful for the exemplary editing skills and support of David Sullivan of the *Philadelphia Inquirer* and for the continued inspiration from colleagues such as Jan Whitaker and numerous friends and fans who have stepped forward through social media sites. I send out a thank-you to Hannah Cassilly and the staff at The History Press, who have stayed with me for six books and counting. And I bow down to my wife, Sandy, who has helped me make book number seven readable through her own sensible and smart editing skills. And, of course, another "shout-out" goes to my daughter, Jordan, the proud owner of a rare "Pomeroy Pebble Person."

INTRODUCTION

Sometimes I wonder if I am the right person to write a book about Pomeroy's. I am not from Pennsylvania, but I grew up in New Jersey, just across the river from Philadelphia. Philadelphia was home to some of the country's most iconic department stores, and its residents had plenty of choices. My mother usually chose Strawbridge & Clothier. That was her store. But every so often, she would put her kids in a station wagon, go for a ride and, for some reason, end up at a Pomeroy's. It wasn't a Philadelphia store and my mother didn't have to go there, but she did. I remember visiting Pomeroy's at a very early age, and I loved the fact that it almost seemed "exotic." (Imagine a kid from the 1970s thinking that Pomeroy's was exotic!) These shopping trips to "exotic" destinations throughout Pennsylvania and New Jersey helped foster my lifelong passion for department stores, as well as their identities and histories. Maybe in the grand scheme of things, I can blame my department store infatuation solely on Pomeroy's.

"Our" Pomeroy's was not in Pennsylvania. It was located in Willingboro, New Jersey, a sole straggler that operated outside the Pennsylvania state line. The Willingboro Pomeroy's anchored a shopping center that served a community formerly named Levittown, New Jersey. The area was strictly blue collar, nothing fancy, suburban and clean—just like the Pomeroy's store, a large, one-story structure that anchored a beautifully manicured shopping plaza. Willingboro Plaza might have been quiet and well past its prime, but Pomeroy's was not. The store usually bustled, and every so often, for no apparent reason, my mother wanted to be a part of that bustle.

After writing a number of books on long-gone businesses—such as Philadelphia's John Wanamaker department stores, the nationally known Gimbels corporation and Washington, D.C.'s stately Woodward & Lothrop—I frequently have been asked, "What store will you be writing about next?" I answer, "Pomeroy's," and the response is usually a blank stare. Pomeroy's does not hail from one of America's glamorous cultural and commercial centers but rather from eastern and central Pennsylvania. Its name doesn't have the cachet and recognition of a Wanamaker's, Marshall Field's or Hudson's.

As I studied and researched Pomeroy's and met former employees and family members, I became extremely fond of this former business. I heard numerous stories about people, such as "Dutch Mary," a madam who paraded her women throughout the Reading store in order to properly dress her staff. Or the longtime and beloved Harrisburg Tea Room waitress named "Mim," who gruffly "welcomed" her customers for decades. Or the blind man who operated a coffee shop tucked away in the Pottsville store and walked eighteen blocks after work to attend evening high school classes. Or the workers from the Wilkes-Barre store who took in homeless employees after Tropical Storm Agnes devastated the city.

I have met some of the warmest, kindest and most generous former "department store family members" as a result of my research of Pomeroy's. This tightknit group of employees and community advocates still keeps in touch and meets from time to time in a variety of settings. There is no Pomeroy's company archive. If it weren't for sharp memories and personalized scrapbooks, this book could not have been written. My work attempts to preserve Pomeroy's proper place in retail and Pennsylvania history.

As I look back at my youth, I still am not entirely sure why my mother took her occasional twenty-mile trips to the Willingboro Pomeroy's. She didn't plan her trips around any special sales and didn't even have a Pomeroy's credit card. Perhaps she just enjoyed getting out of the house, jumping into a car, going for a ride and spending time with her kids. I remember when the Willingboro store shut its doors in early 1987. We all piled into the car for one final trip to Pomeroy's. The store was well picked over and was filled with tables of odds and ends. I'll never forget going up to one table and finding a pair of men's underwear that was a size 60. It was huge, and I regret not buying it as a souvenir. Maybe that pair of size-60 underpants was a reflection of the store—it was a functional item of clothing that was well made and was certainly not "high fashion." That was Pomeroy's.

Chapter 1

PLACING A KEYSTONE

The department store that defined and dominated retailing in eastern and central Pennsylvania for decades began its life as Dives, Pomeroy & Stewart.

Josiah Dives, George Pomeroy and John Stewart were three young clerks at the Brown, Thomson & McWhirtner store in downtown Hartford, Connecticut. The three worked closely together and shared a vision of operating their own dry goods store. Each came from a very different background, but they "dreamed the dream of every ambitious youth, that of owning a business establishment of which they might be proud."[1]

Born in 1851, Josiah Dives was the oldest of the three partners. Dives left his hometown of Canterbury, England, at the age of thirteen and became a salesman at the Debenham & Freebody department store in London. While working at Debenham's, Dives met Hartford merchant James Thomson. Thomson persuaded the young man to relocate to Connecticut. John Stewart was born in Glasgow, Scotland, in 1852. Like Dives, Stewart decided to start a new life in America. He left Scotland in 1874 "shortly after reaching his maturity" and chose to settle in Hartford because of the city's large Scottish population. The youngest of the three men was George Pomeroy. A native of Hartford, Pomeroy was born in 1853 of "Colonial and Continental antecedents" and followed in the footsteps of his father and grandfather, who were successful merchants. The fate of these three young men was sealed when a man named Converse informed them about a business opportunity in Reading. Converse stated that Reading "was a good, substantial farming community, a place with a great future, and that they could make no mistake in starting a store here."[2]

Reading was "a compact city" of forty thousand residents when Dives, Pomeroy and Stewart arrived in the early 1870s. The city was lined with unpaved streets, and its residents struggled with the economic panic of 1873. Market Square, established in 1766 (eighteen years after the city's founding), was the heart of downtown. For most of its life, Market Square was a collection of "unsightly" stalls that required frequent replacement.[3] Reading historian George M. Meiser IX notes that "[Market Square] was lined with open markets but [the city] got rid of it [in 1871] because it became overrun by vermin. The vendors would just throw their food in the streets at the end of the day."

Dives, Pomeroy and Stewart set their sights on the former Mishler & Moers's Globe Dry Goods Store at 533 Penn Street on Market Square. Operated by John D. Mishler from 1868 to 1874, the "cheap" Globe store based its business on quick sales and small profits. "We opened a first-class store, buying the entire stock for cash, thereby saving a large percentage and enabling us to sell lower than those that buy on credit." The Globe Store was frequently attacked for undercutting its competition. Despite initial success, the business ultimately failed. By early 1876, the Globe Building, home to the largest store space in Reading, was in need of a tenant. Dives, Pomeroy and Stewart were quick to secure the property.

On April 1, 1876, Dives, Pomeroy & Stewart opened for business under the Globe Store name but with an "entirely new stock of general dry goods & notions." Their total investment was $1,000. The organizational structure of the business was divided between the three men: Josiah Dives handled the buying, John Stewart hired the staff and George Pomeroy managed the store. Dives, Pomeroy & Stewart introduced Reading to a revolutionary sales concept that eliminated bargaining and haggling. Their policy pronounced, "Same price to all, guarantees always honored, refunds and exchanges cheerfully made, and above all no bargaining!"[4] The store was an immediate success, and the next several years brought major growth to the business. By January 1877, Dives, Pomeroy & Stewart had dropped the Globe Store name since it was no longer needed as a business draw.

In 1878, the three businessmen set their sights on Harrisburg and opened their first branch store. John Stewart was placed in charge of the Harrisburg operation, and the company promoted the same policies there that worked in Reading. Located in the Opera House at 35 North Third Street, Dives, Pomeroy & Stewart developed a loyal following in Pennsylvania's capital city. In 1928, an early customer related her recollections of the first store to the *Harrisburg Telegraph*:

There's one thing I'll always remember about Pomeroy's, when they came
here right from the start, they were always anxious to please their customers.
If you bought a thing and it didn't suit, they did all in their power to make
it right. And that is more than you can say of all the stores of that day, or
any other. But Pomeroy's helped the shopper, and soon the other stores were
forced to do the same.[5]

As the Harrisburg store enjoyed success, it soon became clear that the
current Reading Globe location was insufficient for its growing customer
needs. A larger store, located at 442–44 Penn Street, opened on January 20,
1880, in "one of the airiest and best ventilated store rooms in Reading." The
three-story building housed thirty employees along with a wholesale and
retail operation. But this location's size quickly became woefully inadequate.
The store's popularity "grew to such an extent that for a long time the store
was uncomfortably crowded night after night, and the necessity of a larger
establishment was made apparent."[6]

In 1882, Dives, Pomeroy & Stewart erected a new structure for its growing
business at 606–12 Penn Street. The new department store replaced the
former Aulenbach's Hall. The four-story brick structure with brown stone
trimmings was designed by architect Edward K. Mull and gave "a metropolitan
appearance" to the Penn Square area. One of its most prominent features
was the installation of seven large show windows that displayed the latest
goods. Over the years, the elaborate window displays became a hallmark
and an attraction for the business. The building contained a "cash-ball
system," a "trolley on wires that took cash from the sales counters to the
business office and returned with the proper change."[7] The system improved
efficiency and provided entertainment. Dives, Pomeroy & Stewart moved
into this new home on October 11, 1882. Over the course of four hours
during the previous night, its sixty employees transferred the stock from the
former location. With the opening of its new building, Dives, Pomeroy &
Stewart became the state's largest retail structure outside Philadelphia. As
business grew, the company continued to add on to this structure and the
606–12 Penn Street location formed the original section of the completed
modern-day Pomeroy's store.

During this time, other changes occurred within the business. During
his tenure at the Harrisburg store, John Stewart married Hollie Pomeroy,
George Pomeroy's sister, on August 20, 1880. Within a few years, Stewart
had left his formal duties at the Harrisburg store and returned to Reading.
Reports noted that while living in Harrisburg, Stewart had contracted

GEORGE STRICKLAND POMEROY

Born in Hartford, Conn., July 10, 1853. His family antecedents were Colonial and Continental; he being the son of Joseph and Mary Wadsworth Pomeroy. Mr. Pomeroy doubtless inherited his mercantile tastes from his father and grandfather, both of whom were widely known in the community in which they resided.

Mr. Pomeroy's first step in business was taken when he entered the services of Brown, Thomson & McWhirter in his home city, with whom he remained until 1876, when he joined Mr. Dives and Mr. Stewart in the establishment of the store in this city.

JOSIAH DIVES

Born of English parentage in historic Canterbury, England, in 1851. He was educated in the public schools and also at Cross Academy. A few years after the death of his father, which occurred when he was a lad of 13 years, he went to London to become a salesman in the store of Debenham & Freebody.

In 1872 Mr. Dives was induced by Mr. Thomson, of Brown, Thomson & McWhirter, of Hartford, Conn., to come to America and enter their employ. He remained with the Hartford firm until 1876, when he came to Reading.

Left: This biographical summary of Josiah Dives dates from a 1913 corporate report titled, *Thirty Eight Years of Service—Dives, Pomeroy & Stewart, Reading, PA. Collection of the author.*

Right: The booklet *Thirty Eight Years of Service* also features a photograph and brief informational background on founder George Strickland Pomeroy. There is no known photograph of the third founder of the company, John Stewart. *Collection of the author.*

malaria, which led to pulmonary troubles. In July 1883, Stewart dissolved his interest in the business for $22,000 because of his failing health.[8] Although Stewart sold his share of the business to Josiah Dives and George Pomeroy, the company continued to operate under the familiar Dives, Pomeroy & Stewart nameplate. On November 15, 1885, at age thirty-three, John Stewart passed away from congestion of the lungs. A newspaper report noted, "Intelligent, conscientious and ardently devoted to the business, its personality and connections, the retirement and death of Mr. Stewart fell sadly and hardly upon the surviving members."[9]

Despite the loss of John Stewart, Josiah Dives and George Pomeroy continued to expand the business. Beginning in 1885, the company opened branch stores in Pottstown and Pottsville, in addition to its large stores in Reading and Harrisburg. Business continued to grow in Reading, and the company spent the next few decades adding on to the 1882 structure. Major improvements occurred in 1888, 1892, 1896 and 1898 as the firm added stories, constructed a six-story annex, lengthened sales floors and installed three passenger elevators. By the end of the century, Dives, Pomeroy & Stewart was "the largest and finest department store in Reading, and one of the finest and most complete in Pennsylvania, comprising altogether over thirty distinct departments." The company employed more than 350 workers in its Reading store alone and maintained domestic and international buying offices.

The company was determined to acquire Reading's prime retail corner at Sixth and Penn Streets, the most visible location in the downtown shopping district. The site was home to the Heizmann Building, which included Heilman's Men's Store, Schlechter Jewelers, Orth's Cigar Store and Rote's Restaurant. Initially, the Heizmann family heirs were reluctant to lease the land to Dives, Pomeroy & Stewart. After much deliberation, members of the Heizmann family agreed to lease the property to the department store beginning in November 1899 for a ninety-nine-year term. The agreement called for a seven-story addition that would be regarded as "the first skyscraper in the city and a source of great wonder to the people for many miles around."[10] The department store agreed to have the words "Heizmann Building" engraved at the building's top as a tribute to the corner's former occupant. The lease called for an annual rent of $7,200 over the course of the next ninety-nine years.[11] Historian George Meiser recalls the story surrounding the new lease agreement: "When [Dives, Pomeroy & Stewart] first signed the deal for the Heizmann property, it became good money [for the Heizmann heirs] but over time, it became nothing more than 'peanut money.' But I wondered as a kid, that in 1999, are they going to have to move the building?"

On May 10, 1901, Dives, Pomeroy & Stewart opened its largest addition to date. Designed by architect Alexander Forbes Smith, the new seven-story addition served as a landmark for the "New Reading." Hundreds of shoppers flooded the store, and two large banners proclaimed "Opening Day" and "The Big Store," the company's then-popular slogan. Residents were attracted by the illuminated store and wanted to "tour the interior with its cornucopia of household merchandise." Three large flagpoles on

This image of the Dives, Pomeroy & Stewart buildings in downtown Reading dates from January 16, 1900. In the drawing, the store's main entrance was located on Penn Street, and the company had not yet acquired the Sixth and Penn Street corner location. *Collection of the author.*

Opposite: This image of the downtown Reading store shows the collection of various buildings along Sixth Street that formed the large business, including the store's popular Annex. *Collection of the author.*

the department store's roof towered over Penn Square and accompanied the banners. A large floral horseshoe was placed on the main floor as a gift from the employees. Two ribbons were placed over the horseshoe; one read, "Good Luck," and the other stated, "With best wishes for future success. From employees."[12] Its opening-day advertisement seemed apologetic about the lengthy construction schedule for the project, but the company was proud of its results: "[The construction was] hard and we worked to have everything RIGHT and the BEST, so as to reflect our idea of what a modern store should be, both in its appointments and perfect construction."[13]

By 1901, Dives, Pomeroy & Stewart had defined the role of America's burgeoning department store industry as being "everything for everybody."

A 1987 study on the Pomeroy's building and its historical attributes supported this statement:

> *Inside the new store, Messrs. Dives and Pomeroy reached closer to the ultimate department store goal—a self-contained community in itself, serving all the customers' needs, a microcosm of the city outside. Home delivery service (started back in 1885) and mail order service was expanded. The U.S. Postal sub-station on the premises permitted customers to mail Christmas packages without leaving the building. The package checking desk relieved shoppers of the burden of their purchases, allowing them to buy more than they could carry. The information desk provided schedules on train and*

trolley service, and directed the lost. A two-room store hospital handled first-aid emergencies. The store even had its own fire department, trained to contain a conflagration until the city firefighters arrived.

The 1901 addition included fifteen show windows along Sixth and Penn Streets, one window for each of its departments. By the 1950s, the window displays were changed weekly and were a major attraction for downtown visitors.

Over the next twenty years, the Reading store grew piece by piece as it acquired neighboring properties. Construction on one of the company's last major expansions in downtown Reading began on March 29, 1920. Architect Frederick A. Muhlenberg designed an even larger extension onto the store that gave the building a more unified façade. A spring 2001 article in the *Historical Review of Berks County* noted, "The seventh floor and roofline matched the older façade even more closely, with the same windows between terra cotta columns topped by a cornice and ornamental railing. An electric [Dives, Pomeroy & Stewart] sign on the west end roof created symmetry with an identically styled sign on the Building A roof."[14] In addition to the uniform use of Indiana limestone and ornamental cornice work, the new store's "bank-like main entrance proclaimed solidarity and community respect." The store rightfully adopted the title "Business Heart of Reading."

By the end of 1922, the piecemeal expansions and additions had come to a close. On December 5, 1922, 615 employees unveiled a tribute to Dives, Pomeroy & Stewart in the form of a bronze tablet. The five- by three-foot tablet was located just inside the entrance closest to Sixth and Penn Streets. Designed by Frederick Muhlenberg, the tablet acknowledged the company's "tireless energy, tenacity, and the indomitable will to make the name of Dives, Pomeroy & Stewart synonymous with the highest business ethics." The plaque's inscription best summarized the store's prominence as a Reading institution: "Commemorative of the completion of the new building, a monument to the wisdom, industry and integrity of the founders of this store, the firm of Dives, Pomeroy & Stewart. This tablet is erected by their employees as an earnest of their loyalty and esteem."[15]

Former employee Shirley Becker best describes Pomeroy's and the city that it served: "Reading is a place where blue-collar, hard-working people took pride and made the best of what they had. Everybody worked hand in hand. You respected one another. There was just something magical about Pomeroy's. Pomeroy's was for everybody."

Chapter 2
CAPITAL GAINS

I t is somewhat unclear why Dives, Pomeroy and Stewart decided to look beyond their newly established and successful home base in Reading. From their opening day in April 1876, the three men enjoyed brisk business in Reading and actively acquired additional properties to accommodate the company's growing presence. However, the men decided that there was room for more growth in Pennsylvania and decided to set their sights sixty miles west in the capital city of Harrisburg.

On September 28, 1878, Dives, Pomeroy & Stewart opened its first branch store, in Harrisburg's old Opera House Block. Located at 35 North Third Street, the small store consisted of two long counters—one for notions and one for dry goods—and just a few sales clerks.[16] Store partner John Stewart was placed in charge of the Harrisburg store and was shortly joined by William H. Bennethum, an employee from the Reading store. Bennethum served as manager at the Harrisburg location "for many prosperous and expansive years."[17] Born in Berks County, Pennsylvania, Bennethum was given a leadership role with the company because "he showed marked ability for his work, and he made rapid progress in the [Reading] store."[18] By 1884, John Stewart was maintaining a minimal presence in Harrisburg because of ill health. After Stewart returned to Reading and sold his shares in the company, Bennethum became the Harrisburg's store's guiding force.

The Harrisburg location experienced "hard pulling" (credit issues) at first, but within a few years, sales showed growth and the business required more space.[19] In August 1882, Dives, Pomeroy & Stewart relocated to 334 Market

Street. "The store was wedged in tightly between two other buildings, one another shop, the other the Adams Express Company," recalled an early customer.[20] By 1887, the company had acquired 336 Market Street, and the store engaged in a large reconstruction effort. From June to December 1887, Dives, Pomeroy & Stewart relocated its business temporarily to the former Chestnut Street skating rink near Fourth Street and the Cumberland Valley Railroad depot. The company advertised itself as the "Great Store at the Rink." The conditions were less than ideal. The store was largely open to the elements, and employees reportedly slept on the premises and guarded the goods after hours with guns and watchdogs.

Additional expansions in Harrisburg occurred in 1892, when the company purchased the Adams Express Office at Fourth and Market Streets. Four

After operating out of several different locations through the city's downtown, Pomeroy's Harrisburg store settled at the corner of Fourth and Market Streets. The store's entrance was on the far right side of the Opera House building. *Collection of the author.*

Opposite: The first Harrisburg outpost of Dives, Pomeroy & Stewart was located on the first floor of the city's former Opera House. *Courtesy of the Bon-Ton Stores Inc.*

years later, Dives, Pomeroy & Stewart purchased the Fisher estate at Fourth and Strawberry Streets, along with the Temperance Hotel and the Star Independent Building. The city's largest mercantile transaction to date involved the merger of Dives, Pomeroy & Stewart and the H.S. Williamson store at 326 Market Street. The deal was completed in September 1897 and created Pennsylvania's largest department store outside Philadelphia and Pittsburgh. The business comprised so many buildings that the company stopped listing its address in its advertisements. One article in the *Harrisburg Telegraph* newspaper noted, "The place is so well known that it is not necessary to give the number over the door…The firm fully realizes that the people know whom and where is meant when the name Dives, Pomeroy & Stewart is mentioned."[21]

During this time, the store began to define its customer base in Harrisburg. "Its patrons are from all walks of life, and all receive the same courteous treatment. The rich man's dollar is not any better than the poor man's dime, and the dollar of the one will purchase just as much as the dollar of the other. It is a people's store that caters to the best interests of the people," noted a 1968 company brochure.[22] This philosophy formed the backbone of the company's longtime success in Harrisburg, as well as in Reading and its other future expansions.

Known as "Harrisburg's People Store," Dives, Pomeroy & Stewart was highly regarded for fair business dealings and excellent customer service. Howard Spitalny was a longtime employee and manager at the downtown store. His wife, Lee, recalls, "Howard always called Pomeroy's a 'belly store.' It was positioned right in the middle [in terms of merchandise]."

One of the greatest construction projects in Harrisburg involved the rebuilding of the Dives, Pomeroy & Stewart store in April 1904. The company announced the construction of a five-story department store with a restaurant and waiting room at Fourth and Market Streets. The expansion included greater merchandise offerings, a series of bay windows running from the first through fifth floors and Harrisburg's first fire escape. Like its sister store in Reading, the Harrisburg store featured large display windows that presented merchandise from the various departments and attracted "constantly shifting crowds of spectators."[23] By 1905, additional frontage along Fourth Street had been acquired, and a series of display windows was installed that "gave to the entire floor that abundance of light which is so essential to an up-to-the minute display room." The Harrisburg location featured the cash-ball system, similar to the device used at the Reading store. This change-making device consisted of a "croquet shaped ball, split in half, hollowed out and locked." It traveled between sales clerks and cashiers on an overhead track. In 1908, the ball transitioned into a square box that served the same purpose. The cash-ball system was still in use until the 1950s, along with newly installed cash registers.[24]

Dives, Pomeroy & Stewart hosted its third annual Industrial Exposition in the Harrisburg store in March 1908. The company combined entertainment and education and presented demonstrations of weaving, basket making and ribbon tying, in addition to numerous presentations from local manufacturers. A centerpiece of the exposition was the "Shredded Wheat" exhibit held in the store's basement. Representatives from the National Food Company showed how the food, which was "on the lips of almost every one in Harrisburg," was prepared, from a steamed wheat kernel to the

This image of the Harrisburg store shows its westward growth along Market Street. *Courtesy of the Bon-Ton Stores Inc.*

finished biscuit. During the exposition, the Harrisburg Symphony Orchestra provided live music on the second floor, and more than twenty-five thousand persons passed through the store each day.[25]

By 1910, the store had grown to five stories and extended its floor space from Market Street to Strawberry Street. Dives, Pomeroy & Stewart adopted the slogans "The Heart of Harrisburg" and "Harrisburg's Metropolitan Store."

On September 23, 1915, Dives, Pomeroy & Stewart instituted its first Dollar Day at the Harrisburg store. Originally planned in conjunction with Harrisburg's Improvement Celebration, Dollar Day became a store tradition. Items such as silk umbrellas, carpets, china sets, curtains and corsets were sold for only one dollar apiece. The sale became a regular

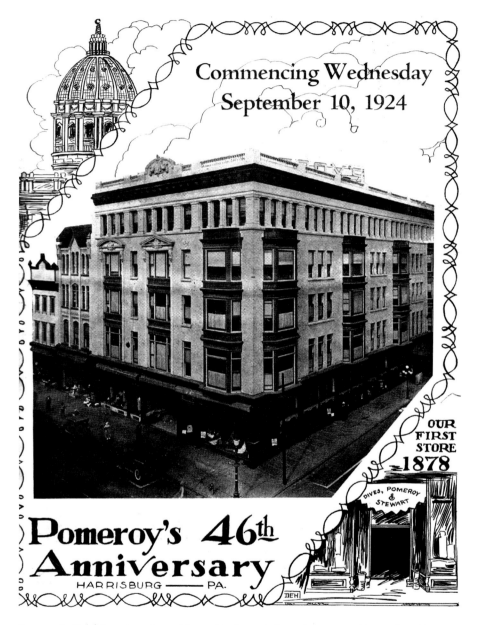

Commencing Wednesday
September 10, 1924

OUR FIRST STORE 1878

DIVES, POMEROY & STEWART

Pomeroy's 46th Anniversary
HARRISBURG —— PA.

Pomeroy's Harrisburg location celebrated its forty-sixth anniversary on September 10, 1924. This souvenir booklet's cover also shows the original Harrisburg storefront in 1878. *Collection of the author.*

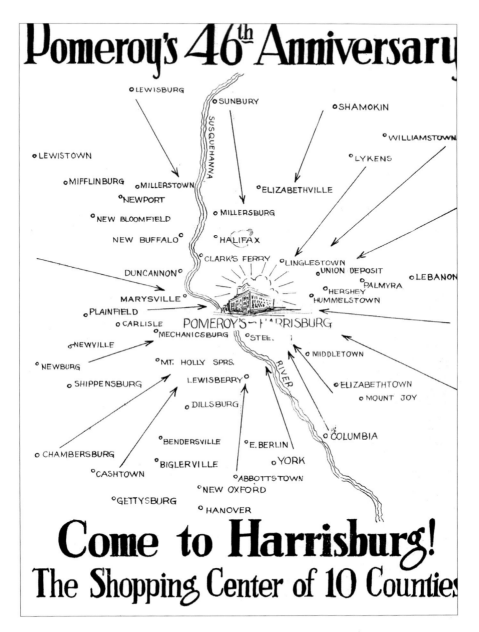

The forty-sixth-anniversary booklet announced that the Harrisburg Pomeroy's store drew from a population base of ten Pennsylvania counties. *Collection of the author.*

promotion throughout the year and cemented the store's reputation for quality and value. In a 1935 advertisement in the *Harrisburg Telegraph*, the company reflected on its humble beginnings:

> *When Harrisburg was a river town, with mud streets and horse cars and market houses in Market Square,* [Dives, Pomeroy & Stewart] *was a one-room shop, with bare board counters and merchandise stacked out front on the pavement. As the city grew, the store expanded. And as Harrisburg now is justly proud of her handsome buildings, her miles of paved streets, her beautiful parks and schools, and business activity, so we too feel honest pride in being "Harrisburg's Greatest Department Store." Recent alterations not only made us one of the most beautiful and modern department stores in Central Pennsylvania, but afforded work for scores of local men.*

After establishing its Harrisburg location in 1878, Dives, Pomeroy & Stewart continued its expansion within Pennsylvania. On March 23, 1885, Dives, Pomeroy & Stewart unlocked the doors of its small Pottstown branch store, located at 256 High Street. The one-room storefront measured just 22 by 120 feet. Within seven years, the Pottstown location had tripled in size. In August 1901, Dives, Pomeroy & Stewart held a massive sale at its Pottstown store in preparation for a major renovation and expansion. The local newspaper reported that "the special sale has been raging like a gulf storm. On Saturday last the receipts doubled any previous day in the history of the store, and a person glancing into the store on Monday and Tuesday might have thought it was Saturday, as there appeared to be no diminishing in the crowds of shoppers."

In 1909, J. Allen Brandt was named manager of the store and later served as the president of the Pottstown Business Men's Association. Brandt was credited for "the progress of the business there since he took charge of it [and] has proven his capabilities as a merchant, his earnestness and aggressive spirit and his deep interest in the work."[26] The upper floors of the Pottstown building housed the Pottstown Business College and the local 814 Elks lodge. Dives, Pomeroy & Stewart operated the Pottstown store for forty-six years until its closure on July 1, 1927. The department store also housed a tea room that continued to be open to diners until December 1928.[27] The Pottstown store closed because it lacked the necessary room for growth, and many of its customers were traveling to the Reading store for its greater selection. The Enterprise Furniture Store assumed the store's lease, and in later years, the building housed Pottstown's J.C. Penney Company branch store.

A rare photographic image of the company's Pottstown store. The Pottstown business operated between 1885 and 1927. *Collection of the author.*

On September 1, 1887, Dives, Pomeroy & Stewart opened its third store—this time in Pottsville, Pennsylvania. Dives, Pomeroy & Stewart purchased the former dry goods business of Jacob Miehle and named Miller as the store manager. The new Pottsville operation, located at 5–7 North Centre Street, was modest in size but formed the basis of the company's long-term success and growth in the small city. Unlike its sister store down the road in Pottstown, the Pottsville location continued to expand in size and sales and eventually established its own separate headquarters. In Pottsville, "the advanced methods of merchandising and the liberal store policy and spirit of aggressiveness of the newcomers and its manager, soon won the favor of the Schuylkill Countians."[28]

In 1893, business "reached such proportions" that the Pottsville store required larger quarters. The company purchased the largest space in Pottsville that could handle the size of a department store, the R.R. Morris building. Over many years, Dives, Pomeroy & Stewart expanded and modernized the

In 1887, Dives, Pomeroy & Stewart established a location in Pottsville. Unlike the Pottstown branch, the Pottsville store expanded greatly over the years and became its own divisional headquarters. *Collection of the author.*

Opposite: An early Pottsville City Directory featured an advertisement for "Schuylkill County's Greatest Department Store." From 1893 until 1983, Pomeroy's Pottsville was located at 100 South Centre Street. *Courtesy of the Historical County of Schuylkill County.*

Pottsville store and remained true to the founders' philosophies, as a store advertisement noted: "[O]ne price to all, guarantees always fulfilled, fullest knowledge given about the goods, refunds and exchanges cheerfully made, and same service to all." The Pottsville store was ranked "with the other branch stores [in the organization] as being the model store of its native city." By 1923, its local Dollar Day promotion passed all previous records.

Although Dives, Pomeroy & Stewart operated four prominent stores by 1887, the company also became a major investor in the William F. Gable Company department store in Altoona, Pennsylvania. William Gable was Dives, Pomeroy & Stewart's very first employee at its Reading store. He spent six years at the Reading business and learned the necessary skills to

become a successful merchant. Gable confided in George Pomeroy that he was interested in starting his own business. Pomeroy knew of an opportunity in Altoona, where businessman John Sprecher was interested in retirement. In 1884, Gable left Reading and moved to Altoona to join the management of the Sprecher & Gable department store. Only three months after Gable arrived, Sprecher retired from the business.[29] The Dives, Pomeroy & Stewart organization purchased Sprecher's interests. The business operated under the Gable name, but George Pomeroy assumed the store's vice-presidency. William Gable "worshipped" George Pomeroy's leadership and friendship to the point of naming his son George Pomeroy Gable.[30] The William F. Gable store was closely tied to the Reading headquarters and utilized many of the Reading store's successful merchandising techniques, creating the "greatest commercial enterprise in central Pennsylvania."[31] By the 1940s, family member Robert B. Gable had begun his tenure as the managing director of Pomeroy's Pottsville location. In 1919, Dives, Pomeroy & Stewart sold its remaining shares in the Altoona store. For decades, Gable's was an Altoona institution that anchored the city's downtown until its closure in 1980, a victim of its parent company's bankruptcy.

Chapter 3

GREATER POMEROY'S

Dives, Pomeroy & Stewart entered the 1920s as a strong, stable business with four successful department stores in Reading, Harrisburg, Pottstown and Pottsville. All four stores served their respective local customers and complemented one another. Founders George Pomeroy and Josiah Dives served as the guiding forces in the business, and the stores enjoyed continued sales growth. Toward the end of the decade, the company experienced another major expansion and a change in leadership.

On September 21, 1922, seventy-one-year-old Josiah Dives passed away after many months of health complications. Dives was regarded as the "master buyer behind the firm's success" and was known for his unassuming personality. Kline, Eppihimer & Company, a Reading retail competitor, published a notice in the *Reading Times* that paid tribute to Dives: "[Dives was] a gentleman of the old school, courteous and kindly, who, in spite of a modest and retiring nature, had a host of friends, and who, through the great business institution of which he was a partner, was known by reputation throughout eastern Pennsylvania." Many notable citizens from Reading and Harrisburg attended his funeral, and all four company stores were closed for three days to show respect for Dives's passing.

Upon Josiah Dives's death, George Pomeroy, the last remaining founder of the business, acquired full ownership of the department store. In August 1923, Pomeroy arranged the purchase of Dives's remaining shares from his heirs. This action changed the store's status from a joint partnership between Dives and Pomeroy to an incorporated business owned solely by

The downtown Reading store fully decorated for the Christmas season—note the snow on the streets. This photograph shows the completed structure at Sixth and Penn Streets, including the store's signature and iconic rooftop sign. *Courtesy of the Historical Society of Berks County.*

George Pomeroy. Pomeroy promised no changes in the store's policies and management structure. In the previous years, Pomeroy had brought his son, George S. Pomeroy Jr., into the store's management, as Dives's declining health had diminished his leadership role. On July 2, 1923, Pomeroy finalized the paperwork, and the store assumed its new name, "Pomeroy's Inc." Its $2.25 million purchase price was the largest real estate transaction in Reading to date and "launched the [modern] Pomeroy era."[32]

Unfortunately, the day he signed the incorporation papers, Pomeroy went into diabetic shock and was rushed to the hospital. He recovered from his hospital stay but slowly turned over the reins of the business to George Jr. A Yale University graduate, George Pomeroy Jr. eventually became the chief executive of the company and worked alongside his father. While a student at Yale, George Jr. and Meade Minnigerode co-wrote the famous "Whiffenpoof Song" in 1908.

George S. Pomeroy's son shared many of the same personality traits. "[The Pomeroy family] never put on any airs," says Pomeroy descendant Barbara Korczykowski. "I don't think I told people that I was a 'Pomeroy' until I had my own job. [When I was younger] I wasn't allowed to tell anyone. My mother didn't want me to brag." Pomeroy heir James Seivers adds, "I can't emphasize how private my great-grandfather [George Strickland Pomeroy] and grandfather [George Pomeroy Jr.] were…The store represented their integrity and sincerity." Family member Kathy Hayden reiterates, "George Pomeroy Jr. was very difficult to know." Seivers also remembers some of his grandfather's feelings toward the department store's operation: "My grandfather [George S. Pomeroy Jr.] did not care for how ladies wore makeup in those days. Whenever Hollywood starlets came to Reading, he would come home and complain about how much makeup the celebrities wore. He thought that [makeup] corrupted women. It was a very Victorian feeling." These views did not hamper Pomeroy's offerings to its customers. George Jr. realized that makeup (and fashion) were essential in running a successful store and let others buy merchandise for the company.

On September 13, 1925, George Pomeroy Sr. passed away at the age of seventy-two. The *Reading Eagle* newspaper called Pomeroy "a man of few words" who "possessed sound business judgment, displayed a remarkable genius for organizing, and was an excellent judge of human nature. A man of vision, he was ever progressive and on the alert to keep the great enterprise which he directed in the very front rank." George Pomeroy was honored by the C.K. Whitner Company, the store's main Reading competitor. Whitner's issued a statement, "It is with deepest regret that we note the death of our fellow merchant, George S. Pomeroy, Sr. With his passing, the last of the pioneers of Reading's Retail Merchants is gone. We extend to his family and store organization our deepest sympathy in this, their irreparable loss and bereavement." The *Harrisburg Telegraph* cited "expressions of regret, for the store's founder was held in the utmost respect and veneration by hundreds of employees throughout the four establishments."[33] Even Gable's in Altoona, a former associated operation of Dives, Pomeroy & Stewart, paid tribute in the *Altoona Mirror*, saying, "Unselfish, cheerful and undaunted, [Pomeroy] was a business builder and a maker of friends, many of whom he won in this city during his frequent visits. Long may his memory remain."

On September 18, 1925, the will of George S. Pomeroy Sr. was filed for probate, and his estate was estimated at more than $1.5 million. Pomeroy left his estate to his wife, Lillie C. Pomeroy; his son, George S. Pomeroy Jr.; and his daughters, Elizabeth H. Pomeroy and Ellen Potts. The department store business was left in a trust that secured the integrity of the store and its future. Pomeroy's will stated, "I desire for the period of the trust a unity of management, with a view to the careful, efficient and profitable operation of the business and the conservation of the cash resources of the company."[34] Even with the last founder's passing, the Pomeroy stores remained strong and played crucial roles and provided extensive services to customers. In Reading, Pomeroy's housed forty-seven departments, from clothing to furniture, along with Reading's leading photography studio, a beauty parlor, a post office, an optometrist, a sewing machine club and a tea room.[35] The Harrisburg store had fashion shows, art exhibits, musical programs, extraordinary window displays, Harrisburg's largest bookstore and the popular mezzanine Tea Room.[36]

In early 1927, Pomeroy's Inc. seized an expansion opportunity in Wilkes-Barre. A prominent department store located on Public Square had filed for bankruptcy protection and was in the hands of receivers. That property originated as Jonas Long's Sons, Wilkes-Barre's first department store. Founded in 1860, Jonas Long's Sons was known locally as "The Big Store." Architect P.J. Lauritzen designed the building, which was completed in 1895. Lauritzen dealt with the "oddly shaped site by creating a dramatic three-story entrance arch to mark the corner and draw in shoppers."[37] By 1900, Jonas Long's Sons described its business as fifty separate stores under one roof.

A number of other Long family members operated different retail establishments throughout the city. Jonas's cousin, Isaac, owned the Isaac Long Store, which shared a Public Square location along with Jonas Long's Sons. In 1917, Jonas Long's Sons put its business up for sale. Long family member and author Bettijane Long Eisenpreis notes, "I have no idea why Jonas Long sold the store to somebody." On February 1, 1917, William F. MacWilliam—a former executive at Fowler, Dick & Walker—The Boston Store—purchased Jonas Long's Sons. The store was renamed MacWilliam's, and MacWilliam operated the store for about ten years. In late 1926, MacWilliam's filed for bankruptcy protection, and Pomeroy's made a $1.5

Opposite, top: This classic image shows the Pomeroy's on Wilkes-Barre's Public Square. The building's archway advertised the store's popular slogan, "Shop Pomeroy's First." Completed in 1895, the building's top spire displayed the letter *J*, a nod to the business's first incarnation as the Jonas Long's Sons department store. *Collection of the Luzerne County Historical Society.*

Opposite, bottom: Employees gather on the main floor of Pomeroy's in downtown Wilkes-Barre soon after the company acquired the MacWilliam's business in 1927. *Collection of the Luzerne County Historical Society.*

million offer for the business. Creditors were guaranteed to be paid in full and the sale was approved. "[MacWilliam's] went through some real grave times," says Eisenpreis. Pomeroy's took possession of MacWilliam's on February 19, 1927. With locations in Reading, Harrisburg, Pottstown, Pottsville and Wilkes-Barre, Pomeroy's enjoyed an expansive presence throughout Pennsylvania.

After it opened its Wilkes-Barre store, Pomeroy's announced that its "prices are moderate and selections are suitable to every one's budget."[38] The company became known as an "all-purpose store" that served many hardworking Pennsylvanians. By the end of 1927, Pomeroy's had closed its Pottstown branch and was concentrating on its "quartet" of large stores. Reading historian George M. Meiser IX says, "Pomeroy's had everything from clothing to pencil sharpeners to the latest novels. No store today has that depth of inventory." Former manager Ross Ricketts states, Wilkes-Barre was "not a high-fashion market, since it was in more of a blue-collar market." Those in the area, with more money to spend, usually traveled to New York or other Eastern cities for specialized designer merchandise.

Pomeroy family member Kathy Hayden reiterates that the family kept to itself and did not talk openly about the retail company. She notes, "[In later years] I went to Wilkes-Barre for business, and I saw the Pomeroy's store and thought, 'Whoa!' I had no idea that there was one up here!" In Harrisburg, "Pomeroy's catered to the middle class," says Lee Spitalny. "The elegant or 'country club set' shopped in Philadelphia or New York." That sentiment was echoed in Pottsville. "Downtown Pottsville was the place to go unless you traveled to Philadelphia or Reading," says Pottsville resident Norma Cresswell. "It was the only place for Schuylkill County to shop." Within the Pomeroy family, certain members also traveled elsewhere for higher-end merchandise. George Pomeroy's great-grandson James Seivers recalls that his great-aunt Ellen married into the famous Reading-area Potts family. "Whenever my great-aunt Ellen Potts had the time to go shopping, she went to New York. But when she needed to shop in Reading, she'd usually buy her clothes at Whitner's."

Chapter 4

ALLIED FORCES

Pomeroy's attributed its early success to affiliations that gave the department store access to international buying offices, popular sales trends and sophisticated marketing assistance. Pomeroy's had the upper hand, as it traded in smaller Pennsylvania cities and persuaded customers to shop closer to home through better selections and competitive price points.

In about 1894, Dives, Pomeroy & Stewart became a member of the New York–based Syndicate Trading Company. Initially, the Syndicate Trading Company was a conglomerate of ten stores that bonded together as a "single organization [that] practically dictated prices." With branch offices in Manchester, Paris, Chemnitz and St. Gall, the Syndicate Trading Company acted as the buying office for its members. Syndicate Trading Company was not involved in the capital, management or selling aspects of its member stores, but in 1900, its buying strength earned it the self-imposed title of "the most powerful mercantile combination in America."

In 1914, Reading played host to the annual meeting of the Syndicate Trading Company's members. It was "the first time a number of [national merchants] had the opportunity to see this city, the surroundings and the big store which makes one of the dozen prominent department stores included under the Syndicate Trading Association," noted the *Reading Times*. At the time, the organization was regarded as "probably one of the oldest mercantile associations in the country" and consisted of member stores such as Bon Marche of Seattle; O'Neill's of Akron; Almy, Bigelow & Washburn of Salem, Massachusetts; Denholm & McKay of Worcester, Massachusetts;

and Brown, Thomson & Company of Hartford, Connecticut. Brown, Thomson & Company was the firm where Josiah Dives, George Pomeroy and John Stewart originally worked and connected together.

The Commonwealth of Pennsylvania was especially hard hit during the Depression years. Before 1929, Pennsylvania boasted the United States' second-largest industrial workforce. However, by 1933, Pennsylvania had lost more than 270,000 manufacturing jobs, the third-biggest job loss nationally. The number of families seeking financial relief topped the country's roll call, more than New York or Illinois, and burdened the state.[39] Reading suffered from the downturn in the textile industry, while the areas surrounding Pottsville experienced the demise of the "coal era." As the home of the state government, Harrisburg weathered the Depression somewhat better than its statewide counterparts but was not unaffected by the economic collapse. Located in the hearts of Pennsylvania's troubled industrial cities, Pomeroy's adjusted its merchandise selections as it faced declining sales figures.

Pomeroy's addressed the economic slump and formally established a "bargain basement" operation. Modeled after larger department stores in major cities, Pomeroy's Basement Store featured discounted merchandise that was purchased by a separate buying staff. The concept was established at the Harrisburg location in early 1928 and in Reading in March 1929. Although all four Pomeroy stores had previously featured basement departments that offered home goods and garden departments, this new development devoted an entire floor to clothing and housewares at affordable price points.

The Basement Store proved to be a popular operation and lasted throughout the store's lifetime. Harrisburg author Florence Ditlow says, "If you only had a few pennies to spend, you'd go to Pomeroy's Basement. That's where you could get last year's dress." Lee Spitalny adds, "The Basement Store was 'crazy-nutzy.' Once there was a basement sale where Pomeroy's bought out the stock of another children's store. Every woman with a child in the city of Harrisburg came to the store. It was like Black Friday; it was like Filene's Basement!" Buyer Pat Eichorn recalls how the ladies' toilets in the basement had ultraviolet lights over the toilet seats: "When you flushed the toilet, the light would turn on to kill the germs on the toilet seats!" Customer Veronica Smith fondly remembers Pomeroy's Basement in Harrisburg. "My sister and I always headed for Pomeroy's Basement when we first started paying for our own clothes!" Historian Ken Frew notes, "They carried a lot of seconds in the basement. It was great as long as you didn't mind wearing undershirts that were slightly irregular." The basement also proved successful at the smaller Pottsville store. "We'd have visitors from Strawbridge & Clothier in

Philadelphia that would come to Pottsville just to shop and check out our basement," says former employee Delores McKenna.

The Pottsville Basement Store was especially popular because it had a direct entryway from the store's front sidewalk. "You could walk right into the basement directly from the outside, down a flight of stairs," says McKenna. "There was a women's comfort station at the bottom of the stairs that had a permanent attendant. You would use the comfort station and walk right into the basement." The basement was also an important feature at the Wilkes-Barre store. Former buyer Mike Carratilo remembers some of the bargain merchandise that was offered there: "I remember that the store would put up four large tables near my office and load them with Playtex girdles that had holes in them that were packed in tubes," says Carratilo. The condition of the bargain merchandise did not matter, as the goods usually sold out quickly.

On September 18, 1934, surprising employees and customers, George S. Pomeroy Jr. announced the purchase of Pomeroy's Inc. by Hahn Department Stores. Hahn was the forerunner of the Allied Stores Corporation, a national holding company that operated well-known stores such as Jordan Marsh in Boston, Donaldson's in Minneapolis and Maas Brothers in Tampa. The purchase price was undisclosed, but the transaction included a generous exchange of stock. "One of the reasons that my grandfather [George Pomeroy Jr.] sold the store was because of economic pressures," notes Pomeroy family member James Seivers. "The store was losing money, lots of money. It was either that or go bankrupt." At the time of the sale, George Pomeroy stated that "in [my] opinion this move would greatly strengthen and help the Pomeroy stores and would prove a real benefit to the company and the communities which they serve."[40] With the purchase of the four Pomeroy's stores, Hahn Department Stores became an organization with thirty-two stores that generated $85 million in sales.

In 1935, amid concerns over its plummeting stock values, Hahn Department Stores was forced to reorganize. "Lew Hahn was just a figurehead," says former executive Lee Starr. "He was a public relations guy and wasn't even an executive. The company just needed a name." After it suffered from some heavy sales losses, the business was reorganized and renamed the Allied Stores Corporation. Allied chose a new operating strategy that combined a "unique blend of chain store centralization and local store autonomy." The new leader of the company was B. Earl Puckett. "[Puckett] was a genius," says Starr. "Puckett saw that Allied was just a jumble of stores [of all sizes], and he organized the company."

Allied relied on a strong central national headquarters that supported and guided local decision-making. Allied stores were divided into regions, and each independent unit had its own managing director and merchandise manager.[41] This new structure affected Pomeroy's. Allied regional director Albert Coons requested that each Pomeroy store report to the New York headquarters. Formerly, the Harrisburg, Pottsville and Wilkes-Barre locations had answered to the Reading management. In addition, Allied established Harrisburg as the regional office that handled marketing and buying functions for the four stores. A number of upper-management positions in Wilkes-Barre, Pottsville and Reading were eliminated. "All of the offices eventually ended up moving to Harrisburg, but it didn't affect the Reading store," says former employee Shirley Becker. "It was still run well." By the end of the 1930s, Allied Stores had reversed the financial woes of the former Hahn organization. Pomeroy's was able to focus on its future, including a full renovation of its Harrisburg headquarters store.

On November 15, 1939, Pomeroy's opened a rebuilt store in downtown Harrisburg. The new five-story building was constructed with an exterior of limestone and glass brick. It was the result of five years of planning under the supervision of managing director Charles A. Holmes. The "New and Greater Pomeroy's" included an air-conditioning system, the removal of extraneous walls, modern display windows, an expansive marquee to protect shoppers from inclement weather and a 20 percent increase in floor space. Holmes stated, "For several years we have worked and dreamed of a new and greater Pomeroy store and now that dream has become a reality. Modern throughout, the new Pomeroy's is one of Pennsylvania's finest department stores. The fulfillment of this vision has been made possible by the good will and confidence of our many friends in Harrisburg and Central Pennsylvania."[42]

In her essay "The Last Words of a Landmark," former employee Lois Witmer recalled the Harrisburg store in its heyday:

> *Over the years, thousands of people were employed here and millions, perhaps billions, of visitors enjoyed the pleasure of shopping sprees and leisurely dining in the mezzanine Tea Room. Fashion shows, art exhibits, musical programs, and extraordinary window displays were forms of entertainment many times over.*

Two of the most prominent sections of the remodeled Harrisburg store were its book department and Tea Room. "One of the most alluring sections of

A new, streamlined downtown Harrisburg store, referred to as "Greater Pomeroy's," reopened to the public on November 15, 1939. *Collection of the author.*

the entire store is the colorful book department which contains the largest circulating library in Central Pennsylvania," stated the *Harrisburg Telegraph.* The book department dated back to the store's earliest days as Dives, Pomeroy & Stewart and was situated toward the rear of the street floor. In later years, the department was relocated to the basement. Author Florence Ditlow remembers the excitement associated with book shopping at Pomeroy's. "You could buy best-sellers right out of the crate for two dollars, even before they became bestsellers and before they were released as paperbacks!"

The mezzanine Tea Room was a culinary and social destination for Harrisburgers. In 1939, the Tea Room became glass-enclosed but still allowed a spectacular view of the main selling floor. Unlike department store tea rooms in other major cities, Pomeroy's Tea Room was simple and down to earth. Ditlow agrees that the Tea Room served many different purposes. "You didn't get a lot of alone time with your mother, so a visit to the Tea Room was quality time," says Ditlow. "My mother spent time in the Tea Room as a kid, and I guess she wanted us to have the same good experience. You could either just sit at the counter or just sit overlooking the main floor surveying the scene." Buyer Pat Eichorn enjoyed looking down at the main shopping floor from the Tea Room because "you'd always see somebody down there that you'd know!" Lee Spitalny's husband, Howard, liked to eat in the Tea Room because "he could look out the glass window at his department to make sure everything looked just right."

Pomeroy's Harrisburg Tea Room was known for sandwiches made with cheese bread and its famous cinnamon sticks. Bettie Hazzard met her husband, Russell, at Pomeroy's in Harrisburg. "Russell was a baker and a short-order cook at Pomeroy's. After working in the paint department, I took a job in the store's pet shop. Russell used to come up to see me in the pet department, and he'd teach my parrot to swear!" says Hazzard. Bettie notes that Russell was responsible for all of the baking, from the cinnamon sticks to the cheese sticks, biscuits and shepherd's pie. From the massive inventory to the special departments like the book department and Tea Room, Pomeroy's duplicated Harrisburg's success at its large Reading store.

Pomeroy's Reading store rivaled the Harrisburg headquarters in size and importance. "Its 47 departments offered everything needed in the home—from clothing, furniture, appliances, and even groceries, to services like Pomeroy's photographic studio, beauty parlor, optometrist, sewing machine club and restaurant," noted an article in a Berks County Historical Society publication. The store's roof was home to radio station WRAW and an official weather station. "A Mr. Richards kept a handwritten log on the city's

Top: One of downtown Harrisburg's most popular eating establishments was Pomeroy's Tea Room. Unlike other American department store tearooms, Pomeroy's restaurants were very casual and affordable. *Collection of Lois Witmer.*

Left: The Harrisburg Tea Room was located on the store's mezzanine level. Diners could survey the sales action on the main floor while they enjoyed lunch. Unfortunately the store's famous cinnamon stick recipe did not survive after the tearoom's closure. *Collection of Lois Witmer.*

weather and was duly noted in book after book," says George M. Meiser IX. According to former manager Ross Ricketts, "The store president had his own office on the eighth floor that had a secret area with its own shower and place to sit in the sun."

Similar to the Harrisburg store, Reading's Pomeroy's housed the city's largest bookstore. The department offered books "originally published at higher prices" and was initially located prominently on the store's street floor. By the 1960s, the company had moved it to the second floor and combined it with the growing record department. Pomeroy's in Reading also featured its own popular Tea Room. The Reading Tea Room, located in the store basement, was "more about sandwiches and short-order food," says former employee Shirley Becker. "Unlike tea room customers in some localities, women here [in Reading] do not insist on the 'superfluous frills' which go into food preparation in similar establishments elsewhere," said Tea Room manager Harry Gissler in 1958. "They like their food to be attractive but they willingly forgo a few extra 'unnecessary touches' in favor of a more reasonable price."[43] Pomeroy's Reading Tea Room was home to the *Breakfast in Berks* radio show, hosted by broadcaster Johnny Deegan on WHUM. The staff of the Reading store utilized an employee dining room that, for many years, was operated through the assistance of the State Council for the Blind and the Blind Association of Berks County. Beginning in 1957, Michael Hawrylko, a blind Readingite, maintained the popular employee lunch vending stand.

In addition to its book department and the Tea Room, Pomeroy's photo studio was well regarded. "Pomeroy's had the city's best commercial photographer," states Meiser. The photographer also worked for the *Reading Eagle* newspaper. "Whenever there was a major story, [the photographer] would put up a sign saying 'Be Back Soon' and go out and take pictures for the *Eagle*." Although they were popular and profitable, the Harrisburg and Reading Pomeroy's department stores never expanded in physical size after the 1930s.

In 1948, the last of the original family members, George S. Pomeroy Jr., quietly retired as managing director of Pomeroy's. During his tenure, George Jr. developed good working relations with his employees. James Seivers recalls, "When my grandfather was president in the mid-1930s, the dockworkers wanted to unionize. He went down to the dock to find out their problems and hear their grievances. He settled the problems without union involvement. It exemplified his abilities to not exert his ego."

Chapter 5
POMEROY DAYS

Along with its revolutionary sales and merchandising techniques, Pomeroy's was a pioneer in providing employee benefit and incentive programs. These offerings helped foster a family atmosphere within the store and between the store's staff and its customers. "We all felt like one big happy family," says former display employee Leonard Miller. "We didn't make a lot of money—but nobody made a lot of money." George M. Meiser IX reiterates, "We were poor and we didn't even know it." Pomeroy's made up for its modest wage packages by providing programs, social and educational, that fostered staff morale and development.

In a 50th anniversary pamphlet from 1926, former advertising manager Ralph Kinsey outlined the many benefits and programs that had been made available to Pomeroy's Reading employees over the past years. These offerings included "employee sick pay after five years of service, educational meetings to help employees 'better themselves,' half-day rewards for reporting to work on time, employee discounts, a store library with over 500 volumes of books, and a stock owning plan that 'few stores give privilege' to their workers."[44] A "first class store paper" called the *Store Booster* was organized in 1914. The paper was "published in the interest of the employees" and gave workers with an "unusual wealth of talent" a chance to contribute articles, but no anonymous contributions were accepted.[45] "I found it fascinating to read in the *Store Booster* that so-and-so was resigning her post as a sixth-grade teacher for the past thirteen years, for a job at Pomeroy's," says Meiser. "The salespeople always had classes available to them, even just for salesmanship.

This postcard scene shows the prominence of the Pomeroy's building in downtown Reading. Other stores seen in the view along Penn Street are Lobel's children's wear store and the W.T. Grant Company variety store. In the background is the popular Sunshine Beer sign ("The Beer with the Built-in Smile"). *Collection of the author.*

Reading's popular Pomeroy Players theater group, under the longtime direction of Ralph Kinsey, poses in a November 1958 photo. *Collection of Leonard Miller.*

It amazed me when somebody noted [in the *Booster*] that they were in their fourteenth year in these courses."

In 1918, the company founded the Quarter Century Club in honor of its employees who had served for more than twenty-five years. Throughout the store's existence, an annual celebration awarded employees a monetary gift and stock option plans. In 1924, 122 Reading employees, 69 from Harrisburg, 16 from Pottsville and 4 from Pottstown earned membership in the club. An article in a *Store Booster* from 1924 noted that "working [at Pomeroy's] for a length of time means something." Pomeroy's also offered its employees recreational outlets for their enjoyment. In March 1925, the Pomeroy Country Club opened near Sinking Spring. More than three hundred Pomeroy employees became members of the club, and a number of those employees enjoyed free lifetime membership. Unfortunately, a fire destroyed the clubhouse only nine months later. It was rebuilt and reorganized as the Green Valley Country Club in 1926.

Ralph Kinsey was best known as the writer and producer of the Pomeroy Players theater group. Established in 1917 at the Reading store, the group consisted of store employees and presented one or two original shows during the year. "You never can tell what talent lies behind the glove counter on the main floor or the stock room in the basement," stated the *Reading Eagle*.[46] The Pomeroy Players appeared in locations such as the Abraham Lincoln Hotel ballroom, the Pomeroy store sixth-floor auditorium and at Northwest Junior High School. Kinsey led the Pomeroy Players for more than forty years, and the theater group continued into the 1960s. The Harrisburg store was home to the Pomeroy Store Chorus. After an initial appearance as the "Carol Chorus" during the 1933 Christmas season, managing director Charles Holmes officially organized the Pomeroy Store Chorus in January 1934. The chorus made frequent appearances during the holidays, at special sales and on WHP and WKBO radio. Dave Shoop frequently accompanied the group of "approximately 30 trained voices comprised entirely of store personnel" on the vibraharp.[47]

These benefits helped shape the retail industry as a whole, and the employees took notice. George Pomeroy and his partners followed in the footsteps of merchants such as Lincoln and Edward Filene and John Wanamaker and applied their business practices to their own smaller markets. Reading employee Shirley Becker remembers, "Pomeroy's treated their employees so well. We had profit sharing, pension, full insurance. We always looked forward to coming to work." In Harrisburg, buyer Carol Brightbill states, "It was a very nice place to work. It was a nice environment.

Unlike today, we had management there for a long time." She applauds Pomeroy's for giving her a chance in a prominent position, especially since women were rarely offered such leadership roles at similar retailers. "I had the opportunity to have a job and be successful at it," she adds. "I didn't go to college, and it gave me the ability to prove myself, have a responsible job and work my way up the ladder."

Wilkes-Barre buyer Mike Carratilo recalls, "It was a great time. It was a friendly group of people who worked hard. The hours were brutal, but if you didn't love retailing, you should never get into it." All Pomeroy divisions in Reading, Harrisburg, Pottsville and Wilkes-Barre shared information. Buyers and managers from all four stores typically met at Allied Stores headquarters in New York for important business meetings. Buyer John Matusek recalls that not all Pomeroy's employees stayed at the same hotel initially. "Some divisions stayed at the Roosevelt Hotel, but others stayed a few steps up at the Paramount. The Paramount was a real 'sleaze bag' hotel." When a new vice-president was hired, everybody from all four divisions joined together at the Paramount. Carratilo says, "We all stayed at the Paramount Hotel in New York on buying trips. After all of the meetings, we'd all go to the bar and have one big party. I'm sure that many important decisions were made the following morning between managers wearing sunglasses and suffering from hangovers."

John Matusek acknowledges the strong attachment that employees had with Pomeroy's: "We had a real loyalty to the store. We weren't paid very much, but we wouldn't go anywhere else." Reading employee Leonard Miller agrees: "I made $27.50 a week as a stockroom worker in 1956. But at certain times, such as the Golden Harvest Sale, executives would give out silver dollars [as a sales incentive] as the employees gathered at the bottom of the escalators." Miller also met his future wife during his time at Pomeroy's. "My wife, Margie, usually worked at Pomeroy's as a 'floater,' and I met her while she traveled from department to department throughout the store." But he didn't need to travel to New York to experience employee bonding. "Every week, the employees would get together on Thursday or Friday nights and go to the Crystal Restaurant. We'd all have a drink and have one big party."

Lee Spitalny's husband, Howard, eventually worked his way up through the company and became manager of the Harrisburg Pomeroy's. "The staff in Harrisburg was a very social group," says Lee Spitalny. "It was a wonderful place to be. I could comfortably walk into the store and know everybody. Howard was an easy kind of boss, even though his office was no bigger than a photo booth!" Spitalny feels that employee satisfaction trickled

A group of Harrisburg employees poses with the store's Santa Claus during one of the group's many social events. *Collection of Lois Witmer.*

A group of Reading employees enjoys a day on the job in the store's camera department. For many years, the camera department was located in the store Annex; it moved to the second floor in 1963. *Collection of Leonard Miller.*

This rare photograph shows an early morning image of the downtown Harrisburg store before the start of a Christmas season. Some of the Market Street display windows are covered by drapes in anticipation of their Thanksgiving unveiling. *Collection of Lois Witmer.*

Pomeroy's downtown Wilkes-Barre store celebrates "Pomeroy Day" as "Wyoming Valley's Great One Day Event"; it featured "Pomeroy's Most Important One Day Event Offers [with] Extra Big Values." *Courtesy of the Greater Wilkes-Barre Chamber of Commerce.*

down to the customer. "At Pomeroy's, you were important. The customer was important when she walked into the store, and that's important in any business." However, this did not mean that the customer was always right. Spitalny recalls one time when her husband was a handbag buyer and a woman came into the store to return a beaten-up handbag. "She told Howard that she had purchased it two days before. Howard told her that she couldn't return it. She went straight up to the manager Phil Hoff's office and said, 'That goddamn Greek isn't going to give me my money back!' Phil said, 'He [Howard] is not a goddamn Greek; he's a goddamn Jew! And I'm a goddamn Protestant, and you're still not getting your money back!'" The employees looked out for one another and treated one another as family. "I loved Pomeroy's. They were great days. Everybody was great and friendly. Nobody was nasty, and there was no hanky-panky [between the workers]," states Harrisburg buyer Pat Eichorn.

The Wilkes-Barre store also enjoyed good relations between employees and customers. "Our customer service made us stand out," says former manager June Bonning. "It was very intense. Our clientele was a mixture of the well-to-do and the regular middle class. We had a good coverage of everybody. The employees stayed forever. You knew who they were even though you might not have known their name." Wilkes-Barre area sales manager Margaret Shipula agrees: "Pomeroy's was an all-purpose store. It was a mediocre store, but not in a bad sense. The clerks were more helpful than at the other Wilkes-Barre stores. They went out of their way for customer service, all the time." Bonning adds, "The customers were dedicated to the store, and the store was dedicated to its customers."

One of the greatest regular sale events celebrated in all four stores was Pomeroy Day. This event was celebrated twice a year, usually in early March and then again in early November, just before the Christmas rush. The company inaugurated Pomeroy Day at the Reading store on March 4, 1933. This initial sale featured "astounding values, astounding savings, and nothing but fine, fresh seasonable merchandise." A radio car that featured the voice of radio personality Polly Pomeroy traveled throughout the Reading area, broadcasting information about the sale. "Preceded by a salute of aerial bombs," the department store released one thousand balloons with attached one-dollar coupons, valid for merchandise anywhere in Pomeroy's. Pomeroy Day in Reading became known as "the sale all Berks County waits for!"[48] The sale did not include discounted or closeout goods. Rather, Pomeroy Day featured "new, wanted merchandise that you'll be wearing for years to come," and the company "spent months and months preparing and gathering these 'top' savings from all the markets of the world."

In Harrisburg, Pomeroy Day frequently displayed the image of a crowing rooster in its Pomeroy Day advertisements. "You will want to get up with the sun to get your share of some of the 'limited quantity' specials" and "You can bet your bottom dollar that it's really something to crow about" were two common advertising slogans. The Pomeroy Day sale in Harrisburg followed four principles: price concessions from manufacturers, group purchases with other affiliated Allied department stores, drastically reduced prices of broken assortments and limited quantity and, finally, sales assurance on all merchandise. Pomeroy Day was a popular sale celebration at the Pottsville store and, along with citywide sidewalk sales promotions, helped draw scores of shoppers to the city's downtown shopping district. "The great store on the square in Wilkes-Barre" also celebrated Pomeroy Day, "Wyoming Valley's Greatest Event of the Year." Wilkes-Barre's buying staff "scooped the market many a time to bring you thousands and thousands of items at genuine savings up to 50% of their regular price."[49] A 1948 advertisement for the Wilkes-Barre sale reminded customers to "Shop Pomeroy's First."[50]

Many customers viewed Dollar Day as Pomeroy's greatest sales promotion. "People would line up outside the Sixth Street doors and almost break them down," says Reading employee Shirley Becker. "We had doorbusters where the store sold twenty bars of Ivory soap for a dollar. It was excitement. Customers looked forward to the sale, and they'd run! Dollar Day happened no more than four times a year, and it was Pomeroy's way of giving customers a [financial] break." Leonard Miller echoes Becker's sentiment: "On Dollar Days, people really almost busted down the doors. Ladies would fight over the cheap merchandise because there was only a limited amount of it." In Harrisburg, employee Bettie Hazzard enjoyed a different sales promotion. "My favorite sale was our 88¢ Gadget Sale," says Hazzard. "People just lined up to buy kitchen gadgets like can openers and strainers. Pomeroy's was just a great downtown general store." Before its Anniversary Sale, employees would dress up and put on a show for sales motivation. For employees only, the play was usually held on the steps to the mezzanine. Lois Witmer recalls another employee tradition: "We always had an 8:00 a.m. Christmas party [on Christmas Eve] where we'd also perform a skit. I wrote the whole thing. I was also the storyteller and recruited people for the parts."

Pomeroy's was also known for its community-minded events. In Wilkes-Barre, the store offered a variety of civic and educational programs to its patrons. "The store had a community room that was offered to customers

The Pottsville Pomeroy's Inc. store promotes a Father's Day celebration along with a message to support the American Cancer Society. The sign asks shoppers to "Mail your gift to 'Cancer, care of your local post office.'" *Courtesy of the Historical Society of Schuylkill County.*

free of charge," says former manager June Bonning. "Pomeroy's sponsored a teen group where they were taught manners and had numerous fashion shows and special events like Red Cross CPR demonstrations." Former Reading manager Ross Ricketts cites one of the store's innovative community events: "We had tables set up throughout the home department where each [nonprofit] group decorated their own table. Customers voted, and the best-looking table setting won a donation to their organization."

These little touches endeared Pomeroy's to its loyal customer base. In Harrisburg, former shopper Veronica Smith remembers, "I just loved Pomeroy's. It was the best store ever. We found everything there, and when we went to Pomeroy's, we were on a mission!" For author Florence Ditlow, other stores didn't have the same feel as Pomeroy's. "There's that feeling you get when you're shopping and you forget time," she said. "You forget to look at your watch, and an hour would slip away. The store wanted you to get into that mindset. Maybe it was the nice people who worked behind the counters, or maybe it was that you knew the store layout in your head? Whatever it was, Pomeroy's was just a place that made you feel good."

Chapter 6

EVER CHANGING, EVER INTERESTING

Whether one lived in Reading, Harrisburg, Pottsville or Wilkes-Barre, residents looked forward to elaborate window displays and Christmas decorations at their local Pomeroy's. Josiah Dives, George Pomeroy and John Stewart believed in the power of advertising. Especially in its earlier years, the company was noted as the largest advertiser in its respective local newspapers. Its promotions and displays helped set the store apart from the competition.

Before the 1900s, early department stores concentrated on selling merchandise rather than providing entertainment with decorations and promotions. In 1890, James Edgar became the country's first department store Santa Claus. As the owner and operator of Edgar's Department Store in Brockton, Massachusetts, Edgar wore a red suit, inspired by a Thomas Nast drawing from 1862, and welcomed young and old customers into his large store. "Without Edgar's persona, millions and millions of happy memories may have never been a reality," stated Brockton businessman John Merian.[51] By the 1920s, Santa Claus was a popular fixture at most department stores. His presence guaranteed a steady flow of young customers and their parents into the department stores during the all-important holiday buying season. Large stores needed to find the perfect person to portray Santa Claus. In October 1950, Pomeroy's placed a classified advertisement in the *Reading Eagle* newspaper that looked for a "stout middle-aged man who was in good physical condition and liked children."[52]

On December 13, 1908, an article in the *Reading Eagle* newspaper detailed the decorations on Dives, Pomeroy & Stewart's main sales floor: "[Pomeroy's] long aisles were arched with holly and hung with red Christmas bells. There were beautiful articles upon every counter. The toy room is by far the most charming spot in all the place…Kris Kingles [*sic*] holding their tiny trees—the Tannenbaum of Germany—bringing with them the story of the Yuletide."[53] By 1920, Santa Claus was a regular fixture at the Reading Pomeroy's Toyland, "a gay, gleeful land brimming with many new, modern toys, and all the old favorites." Originally located on the second floor, Toyland eventually took up residence on the store's sixth floor. During the year, the sixth floor was not open to customers. It housed storage and the employee lounge, but that changed on the day after Thanksgiving. "The sixth floor was unbelievable. It was a wonderland," says George M. Meiser IX. "We had a merry-go-round, pony rides…there was just a lot of stuff going on," adds display employee Leonard Miller. "We started working on the animated figures in July. We decorated the store from the top down. By November, we would be ready for the main floor," says Miller. "Jim and John Luft were master puppeteers, and they came in to do the Christmas windows," recalls Meiser. "They were bright, very artistic men who were just incredible. Everybody was dying to see what they'd come up with for Christmas!"

Toyland in the Reading Pomeroy's was a holiday destination for generations of shoppers. Store employees, such as Leonard Miller and Shirley Becker, enjoyed a sneak preview of Toyland a few days before it opened to the public. Miller cites the well-known Fish Pond, where children could fish for a surprise gift, and Becker remembers Toyland for "its beautiful toy displays and mechanized rides; the popcorn, hot dogs, cotton candy and other snacks and drinks; and the requisite chat with Santa, with whom you could have your picture taken."[54] Dozens of different Readingites performed as the "Real Santa Claus," including boxing announcer Harold L. "Runt" Runyeon, sports legend Harry "Cy" Young and Herman L. Holtzman. When once threatened by a youth with a gun, Holtzman said, "I'm not scared. Go ahead and shoot me." The child fled the store.[55]

Pomeroy's Santa was always the guest of honor at Reading's Christmas Parade, held the Saturday before Thanksgiving, and the procession always ended at Sixth and Penn Streets, where Santa climbed a fire ladder into the window of Pomeroy's Toyland. George Meiser says, "Reading was an absolutely glorious place. I remember Christmas shopping on Penn Street as a kid. Two weeks before Christmas, the sidewalks were so full that you had to walk in the street!"

The small Pottstown store, which operated from 1885 to 1927, has the earliest record of a Pomeroy Santa Claus. A 1972 article in the *Pottstown*

Pomeroy's advertises Santa's arrival to the Reading store in 1964. Santa started his visit on the mezzanine level before he traveled to the famous sixth-floor Toyland. In this advertisement, Pomeroy's promotes six different Toylands in the Reading store: Doll Land, Wheel Land (bicycles, wagons and scooters), Science Land (scientific toys and games), Craft Land (do-it-yourself projects), Adventure Land (toys from the "exciting frontier days") and Play Land (indoor games, building sets and puzzles). *Collection of the author.*

Mercury newspaper recalled, "In 1899, however, there were plenty of children who didn't know the awful truth about two Santas; one from each of Pottstown's leading stores, Dives, Pomeroy & Stewart and Cookerow's Shoes, were carefully listening to the toddlers' requests." Pomeroy's, located on the south side of High Street, between Charlotte and Penn Streets, filled its windows with toys. The store also placed decorations on its outside hitching posts. Santa Claus was a popular Christmas figure in Pottstown, but many longtime Pottstown residents thought of Raggedy Belsnickel as their holiday persona. Dressed in rags and wearing a mask, Belsnickel brought gifts to Pottstown's well-behaved children and frightened children who had been disrespectful to their elders.[56]

Pomeroy's Harrisburg store was also well known for its own Toyland, complete with ten-cent pony rides (plus a one-cent tax). In addition to the second-floor toy department, Pomeroy's Christmas display windows were a Harrisburg tradition. "During the 1940s and 1950s, as the holiday season approached, [the] windows would come alive with mechanical people and/ or animals," recalls Harrisburger Lois Witmer. "All the adults who peered into them became children alongside of their own. Seeing all those big sparkling eyes filled with amazement gave the Christmas season as extra glow of warmth." Employee Mary Custer states, "They would frequently bring in windows from the big New York stores that were shown the previous year."

Pomeroy's always unveiled its windows during Harrisburg's annual Yuletide Parade. "[Pomeroy's] windows were great," says historian Ken Frew. "You couldn't even walk down the sidewalk!" A 2005 article in the *Harrisburg Patriot-News* described the thrill of Christmas in downtown Harrisburg: "The sights, the sounds, the spirit, the lavish gift displays, Santa's toyland, the model railroads at Joe the Motorists' Friend on Market Square, those wondrous animated characters in Pomeroy's windows, voluminous shopping bags stuffed with packages, and, yes, even the crowds got everyone in the holiday mood." Employee Pat Eichorn remembers one special Christmas season tradition: an American Indian would sit on the main floor surrounded by children, who formed a tight circle. "He'd sit in the middle with all types of feathers and Indian goods for sale. It was very popular." But, as the *Harrisburg Patriot-News* noted in 1992, "if it is never remembered for anything else, Pomeroy's will be remembered for its Christmas windows."

Throughout the year, the show windows at the Wilkes-Barre Pomeroy's were much more sedate than those of its department store competitors. "I even noticed as a kid that Pomeroy's show windows were minimalistic," says Wilkes-Barre historian Tom Mooney. "They had plain backgrounds and just a few models and items to suggest what was inside." However, the Wilkes-Barre store celebrated the holidays with more elaborate designs, often featuring mechanized displays located up on the store's second-floor arch overlooking Public Square. Even Easter decorations featured mechanical displays on the outside canopy. A large mechanical egg opened and closed and revealed bunnies, flowers and other Easter scenes.

The Pottsville store was smaller than the Reading or Harrisburg locations, but it rang in the holidays with more plentiful goods and festive window displays. "We crammed a lot of merchandise into that store," says former

Above: Shoppers crowd Harrisburg's Market Street during a Christmas season in the 1940s. This photograph shows the Woolworth and Bowman's storefronts and a banner for Pomeroy's as "The Christmas Store." *Courtesy of the Historical Society of Dauphin County.*

Left: The Pomeroy's Pottsville store is decorated for the Christmas season, advertising sale prices for "galoshes" and "rubbers." *Courtesy of the Historical Society of Schuylkill County.*

Display employee Leonard Miller poses in the Reading store's second-floor housewares department. *Collection of Leonard Miller.*

Opposite, top: This Reading show window advertises Pomeroy's February Furniture Sale in the late 1950s. The store's furniture department was located on the fifth floor. *Collection of Leonard Miller.*

Opposite, bottom: Display employee Leonard Miller poses in the front display window during an annual February Furniture Sale promotion. *Collection of Leonard Miller.*

managing director Lee Starr. "The basement was filled at Christmastime with extra merchandise, like toys, which were not available during the year," remembers Pottsville resident Norma Cresswell. Pomeroy's animated windows were the centerpiece of Pottsville's Centre Street shopping district. "During the holiday season, the crowds in front of Pomeroy's windows were four and five deep," states former employee Lois Gray. Resident Jean Dellock recalls, "The windows had puppets, and there were tall poles outside of the store that were always decorated." Delores McKenna briefly worked at the Pottsville store and noted, "Pomeroy's was a very nice store, and its first floor had some very elaborate counters. The windows were always very attractive, but they weren't the kind that you saw when you took the train to Philadelphia at Wanamaker's." Downtown Pottsville rarely suffered from snow removal issues during the busy holiday season. Steam from a central plant carried warm air throughout an underground pipe structure. This warmth helped keep the streets and sidewalks free from snow and ice.

In Reading, customers who arrived through Pomeroy's Sixth Street entrance chose a set of stairs that took them up to the first floor or down to the basement. For a number of years, Pomeroy's placed a live Christmas tree in that stairway. "One year, the tree caught fire the day after Thanksgiving," remembers former display employee Leonard Miller. "The sprinkler system went off near the Sixth Street entrance and in the basement. That was the last year of the tree."

Pomeroy's changed its window displays in all four store locations every week. "One time, we held a furniture sale, and I placed a male mannequin in a nice robe amongst a bedroom display," says Miller. "On top of the chest of drawers were his hat and sunglasses. Our advertising manager made me remove the display because he felt it was too 'suggestive'!" Miller looks back fondly of his time at the store. "I'll go into places, and people will stop and say that I look so familiar. Eventually, I will say that maybe it could have been from Pomeroy's. People would always see me working in the windows, and Pomeroy's had a lot of windows!"

Chapter 7
AROUND TOWN

R etailers have never been immune to competition. Before out-of-town discount stores and other retailers came to town, department stores faced their toughest competitors just a few blocks away. Pomeroy's enjoyed being the dominant retailer in most of its markets, but its stature was not due to lack of effort. Pomeroy's did not necessarily concentrate on carrying the finest goods; it concentrated on having the broadest selection of merchandise. Downtown department stores usually reached their peak in sales in the mid-1950s, before shopping centers with late hours and vast amounts of parking literally paved the way for increased competition for all local retailers. Any story of a department store cannot be properly told without paying tribute to the competition that fought for higher sales figures but traded and worked as friends behind closed doors.

HARRISBURG

As Pomeroy's promoted itself as "Harrisburg's Greatest Department Store," Bowman's was "Harrisburg's Own Store." This slogan was a nod to Pomeroy's association with Reading and other Pennsylvania cities. Bowman & Company was founded in 1871 and later settled in the 300 block of Market Street. The store offered employee perks such as profit-sharing programs and early closings on many weekdays and Saturdays. In 1951, Bowman's opened its first branch at Kline Village, followed by stores in West Shore Plaza, Sunbury, Pottsville and Danville. A large store in the Capital City Mall opened in August 1974.

For a number of years, the company's slogan was, "When it's bought at Bowman's, it adds to the distinction of your gift."[57] Lee Spitalny, the wife of former Pomeroy's Harrisburg manager Howard Spitalny, recalls Bowman's as a nice store. "It had a good look and feel. Bowman's was just a ¼ inch more of a step above Pomeroy's. Pomeroy's was a busier store than Bowman's, at least that's what I thought because Pomeroy's was our store." Pomeroy's buyer Carol Brightbill has strong feelings about its competitor. She notes, "Bowman's mix might have been better than ours, but it didn't do the volume that we did. As buyers, we used to ride the train to New York together with Bowman family members. I remember some of them being young and arrogant." Harrisburger Bettie Hazzard felt that "you had to be dressed up to go to Bowman's."

By 1976, time had caught up with Bowman's. The company wanted to become part of downtown's new Strawberry Square project, but the firm was bleeding money. In March 1976, Bowman's closed the early Kline Village outlet, and the downtown Market Street location fell next. On April 24, 1976, the doors were locked for good at Bowman's downtown store. The company filed for Chapter 11 bankruptcy the following July, and all stores were closed by 1977. That same year, there was one final attempt to reopen and operate the former Hershey Department Store as Bowman's of Hershey. It lasted until June 1981, when the Harrisburg retailer's legacy was finally put to rest.[58]

Bowman's was Pomeroy's strongest department store competitor in Harrisburg, but another fashionable and famous retailer warrants special mention. Although it was clearly not a department store, Mary Sachs was the go-to store for Harrisburg's upper-end customers. Mary Sachs opened her specialty boutique in 1918 as Harrisburg's "little piece of Fifth Avenue." Sachs was described as "having the pluckiness of a Lithuanian immigrant who went into business on a shoestring budget augmented with a merchandising philosophy driven by customer satisfaction, not sales."[59] In a 1943 interview, Sachs said, "I believe in fine clothes, and by that I do not mean the most expensive or the most extreme styles. I mean the finest quality of line and material and those dateless styles which will give service and pleasure through many seasons."[60]

The original store was destroyed by fire on February 11, 1931, and a new stone and steel structure opened on March 26, 1932. "When I first came to

By the mid-1970s, downtown Harrisburg was no longer perceived as "Central Pennsylvania's Shopping Center." This undated photograph was taken during a Christmas season in the 1970s. Bowman's, Doutrichs Men's Store and one of Pomeroy's Market Street entrances can be seen in this image. *Courtesy of the Historical Society of Dauphin County.*

town, I showed up [to Mary Sachs] in my gloves and hat and her assistant introduced herself to me," says Lee Spitalny. "Her assistant said, 'You're new. Would you like to open a charge account?' I thought that I'd died and gone to heaven." Spitalny clearly remembered Mary Sachs as a "Merchant Princess." She recalls, "Mary Sachs had such a presence. She was very philanthropic. She was short but chubby. You always knew when she was around. She let herself be known. She worked hard. She decided to be a success, and by damn she was." In October 1968, the specialty store, which had expanded to include men's and children's clothing, was sold to Hess's of Allentown, Pennsylvania. It was an attempt for Hess's to diversify its holdings. Under Hess's leadership, the store's image suffered, and the Mary Sachs store was closed on September 2, 1978. It was the end of a downtown fashion icon and gave affluent shoppers one less reason to travel into the city. Many people who shopped at Mary Sachs purchased items for special occasions and were not necessarily regular customers. As native Harrisburger Veronica Smith puts it, "I liked Mary Sachs, but I loved Pomeroy's!"

POTTSVILLE

If there was one market where Pomeroy's dominated, it was Pottsville. Located about one hour northwest of Reading, Pottsville is the county seat of Schuylkill County. Pottsville is the home of Yuengling Beer, the oldest brewery in the country. For many local citizens, Pottsville was "the big place" and "the only place for Schuylkill County to shop." City officials cited the shopping section along Centre Street as "one of the liveliest, most bustling business districts in the nation." Pomeroy's was the city's major retailer, but other retailers, especially specialty clothing stores, supplemented Pomeroy's offerings.

A 1948 study showed that Pottsville, with a population of twenty-four thousand, was home to five department stores, seven jewelry shops, nine shoe stores, eleven furniture stores and thirty-seven clothing shops, in addition to seventeen barbershops and twenty-two beauty salons. Pomeroy's largest competitor was Sears, Roebuck, located directly across from the department store. Sears was smaller in size but carried "a lot more home items." The only large, locally run competitor to Pottsville's Pomeroy's was S.S. Weiss Inc. S.S. Weiss promoted itself as a "popularly priced" or "off priced" department store and operated mostly as a ready-to-wear clothing retailer.

In the late 1960s, the S.S. Weiss store was sold, purchased by the Harrisburg-based Bowman's department store company. Bowman's tried its luck on the 13–15 Centre Street property, across from Pomeroy's, but retreated after only a few years. National retailers such as Kresge, Woolworth and W.T. Grant lined Centre Street, and specialty stores like Knapp's Leather Goods were important Pottsville destinations. "Knapp's was an extra-special store that carried expensive items like purses and gloves," says resident Norma Cresswell. Caster's was a family-run ladies' shop that "would get you anything that you want," recalls Cresswell. "You would just show them a magazine, and they'd get it!" Skelly's and the Grace Shop brought more exclusive merchandise to Pottsville shoppers.

Still, in the end, Pomeroy's was the main store, with a broad selection of clothing, cosmetics, jewelry, furniture and appliances. The company's affiliation with the national Allied Stores Corporation helped bring innovative and desirable products to the small city and raised Pomeroy's stature. Pomeroy's was part of the equation for a night out in Pottsville. "On Saturday nights, you would start out at Pomeroy's, go to the movies and then head for the Pottsville Club, the Elks Lodge or the Lieder Club," says former employee Dolores McKenna. Norma Cresswell agrees. "On Saturdays, there was so much going on there that it was like being in a big city. The sidewalks were crowded, and so were the stores."

WILKES-BARRE

Of its four locations, Pomeroy's experienced its greatest competition in downtown Wilkes-Barre. Pomeroy's was one of at least four large stores that vied for Wilkes-Barre's shopping dollars. The department store benefitted from its large, distinctive building on Public Square. "[The importance of Public Square] was more about what was located around it than the square itself," says Bettijane Long Eisenpreis. Most of the city's business was handled within one block of the square. "If you were on the first block off of the Square, you were okay. You only went beyond that because you were just wandering," says Eisenpreis.

Two brothers, Henry and Asher Lazarus, established the Lazarus Store in 1889. Over the years, its business grew, and in 1928, it moved into a fifty-thousand-square-foot building on South Main Street. The Lazarus

Store enjoyed a longtime affiliation with the national department store organization Mercantile Stores Company. Mercantile operated dominant stores in smaller American cities, such as the Lion Store in Toledo, Joslins in Denver and the Jones Store Company in Kansas City. In 1945, the Lazarus Store warranted further expansion and added a lower level and a third floor.[61] The company promoted itself as "the family fashion center of Northeastern Pennsylvania," but some residents referred to it as the "Little Engine that Tried."[62] The store was located two blocks off Public Square and lacked the walk-by traffic that the other large stores enjoyed. But the store prided itself on quality clothing and exemplary customer service.

The *Times Leader* newspaper defined Lazarus as "a store that made up for its lack of glitter and less-than-modern facility with a sales force known for going just one step further to make the customer happy."[63] Bettijane Long Eisenpreis remembers Lazarus as "more of a second- or third-rate store," and Pomeroy Wilkes-Barre buyer Mike Carratilo saw Lazarus as "a very small, nothing store." Carratilo says, "They didn't have the physical space, and they didn't carry a lot of goods. You'd walk into the store and say, 'Where's the merchandise?'" In April 1979, Lazarus expressed interest in moving its store to Public Square. The proposal included a new multi-level building with an adjacent parking structure. In September 1979, the plan fell through, and the firm decided that it would renovate the current building and reconfigure the store with "new floors, new ceilings and a new efficient layout."[64] Despite the announcement that it would turn the operation into a "first-class department store," Lazarus's owner Mercantile Stores Company called it quits on its Wilkes-Barre division. Mercantile felt that it could not continue with its declining sales figures.[65] On January 3, 1980, the Lazarus Store opened its doors for a final liquidation sale. Thousands of shoppers jammed its aisles as store security controlled and monitored the store entrances. Its closing shocked downtown businesses and supporters, and some predicted that the closing of Lazarus would "kill downtown Wilkes-Barre."

One of Wilkes-Barre's finest retailers joined Pomeroy's on Public Square. The Isaac Long Store was founded on South Main Street in 1873 but moved its growing business to Public Square's Welles Building in 1891. Isaac Long's was the smallest of the city's department stores. Located in a "turn-of-the-century dark brown building," Isaac Long's catered to Wilkes-Barre's upper-class customers. As a student, John Maday was employed in the store's china and gift wrap departments. "Isaac Long's was high end. You could tell that these folks never went into Lazarus," recalls Maday. The five-story department store was expanded and fully renovated in May 1963, including "a coating of white paint, a new display layout and an attractive new sign [that] gave the impression of cleanliness and brightness."[66]

Scranton's Cleland Simpson Company, operator of the Globe Store, purchased Isaac Long's in 1965, and John Wanamaker of Philadelphia subsequently acquired the Globe Store on August 21, 1968. The Isaac Long Store was devastated during the massive Hurricane Agnes flooding in June 1972. Wanamaker's declared the business a total loss and chose not to reopen the store. "I recall that my father worked at Isaac Long's until it closed in 1972, due to the flood," notes historian Tom Mooney. "He had to find another job [after the flood]." The devastated Isaac Long Store building was finally demolished in late 1974.

Pomeroy's strongest competitor in Wilkes-Barre was Fowler, Dick & Walker—The Boston Store, originally founded in 1879 by George Fowler, Alexander Dick and Gilbert Walker. The store's complicated name was a combination of the founders' names, as well as an acknowledgement to the Boston wholesale merchants who supported the business in its infancy.[67] After establishing the business on "Wood's Block" in Wilkes-Barre, Fowler, Dick & Walker opened stores in Binghamton, New York; Glens Falls, New York; Lafayette, Indiana; and Evansville, Indiana. By the mid-1940s, the Boston Store had grown to include five floors, five hundred employees and 250,000 square feet of retail space. The company installed an "ultramodern" plaid-pattern storefront in 1961 and built two rear parking decks in 1965. In 1973, the Boston Store opened its only branch store, located at the Laurel Mall in Hazleton. The department store was a formidable competitor to Pomeroy's and, though it offered merchandise of similar quality, was usually regarded as Wilkes-Barre's dominant retailer. "At the Boston Store, you would see the same faces year after year," says John Maday of the Greater Wilkes-Barre Chamber of Commerce. "Their employees became part of the 'wallpaper.' It was tough getting around the store without talking to people." The Boston Store became popular for its "Thrifty Thistle Days" sales and was known as "A Great Store in a Great State" and a place to "park, shop and eat."

The Boston Store remained in family hands until May 1980, when Frank Burnside, a descendant of George Fowler, sold the company to local businessman Ken Pollock. Three months later, Pollock sold Fowler, Dick & Walker—The Boston Store to Boscov's Department Stores. "We bought it on a Thursday and had a grand opening on Sunday," says Chairman Albert Boscov. "We didn't have much time, but we fixed it up the following year." Boscov's arrival indicated a new commitment to downtown revitalization and was praised by Wilkes-Barre. Former Pomeroy's cosmetics manager

Mike Carratilo calls Albert Boscov "the smartest retailer that ever lived" and recalled one of Albert Boscov's initial policy changes at the Boston Store in particular. "The Boston Store had coin-operated pay toilets in the men's and ladies' rooms," notes Carratilo. "The first thing Al did was he removed the coin machines. Al made sure that his customers would not have to pay to use the bathroom at Boscov's!"

Boscov decided to keep the Boston Store sign on the Main Street frontage in addition to the Boscov's name. "The Boston Store was there forever," states Boscov. "It was tradition; why should we change it? [At the time of the store's founding] all good imports came from Boston—at least that's what we were told." Even today, as most stores have closed, merged or changed names and identities, the former Boston Store remains open, a symbol of downtown Wilkes-Barre's strength. Boscov's is committed to its Wilkes-Barre location, even though its home and corporate headquarters are located in Pomeroy's original hometown of Reading.

READING

One year after the founding of Dives, Pomeroy & Stewart, Calvin K. Whitner opened his first-floor storefront at 433 Penn Street on April 14, 1877. Beginning in 1883, Whitner's started expansion construction, and its four-story emporium was completed in 1910. Unfortunately, on May 25, 1911, the building was destroyed in a spectacular fire. Whitner's described its "misfortune" in a newspaper advertisement that noted, "Even while Thursday night's fire raged, instructions were issued toward making the best possible of the conditions in which we found ourselves, and toward re-establishing our modern concern in the city [Reading] as one of the foremost of the big stores."[68] The company wasted no time with its rebuilding efforts. Whitner's had the site cleared within one week and reopened its new building on October 14, 1911. The *Reading Times* called the effort "an inspiring example of promptitude, energy and efficiency…[C.K. Whitner] has set a new pace for Reading and given emphatic proof that the city is not nearly as slow as it appears."

Whitner's became a formidable competitor to Pomeroy's and offered a different level of goods to Readingites. "Whitner's was a cut above," says Pomeroy's display employee Leonard Miller. "Its windows were classy; the

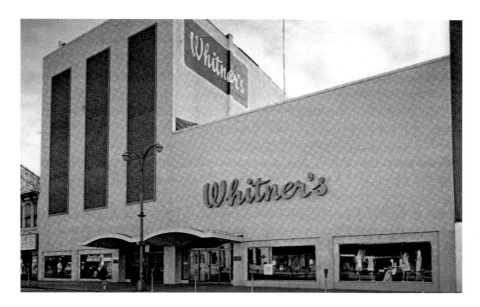

This postcard shows the Penn Street frontage of Whitner's downtown Reading department store. This scene shows the 1967 modernization of the building's exterior. *Collection of the author.*

whole store felt old, quiet and classy. It had the atmosphere of a Lord & Taylor." The store catered to Reading's upper-middle class, and chauffeurs frequently waited outside the store while their passengers shopped for goods. As did Pomeroy's, Whitner's offered a tea room, but it was more formal than its competitor's. "Whitner's had the most wonderful café and dining room," recalls former Pomeroy's employee Shirley Becker. "Its tearoom employed these little old ladies who cooked meals that were all homemade. They were there as long as I can remember."

Whitner's installed Reading's first escalator service on August 21, 1948. Crowds descended on the store to experience this innovation. Prior to its escalator installation, Whitner's had only provided two passenger elevators for upper-floor access. George M. Meiser IX notes, "Whitner's got the first escalator in the city just in time for the city's bicentennial, and it was a big deal. You didn't see a lot of kids in there [before the escalator installation] unless they were being dragged along by their mothers!" John Whitner Rick, great-grandson of C.K. Whitner, cut the ribbon and was the first person to ride the new electric stairs. "[Alfred Lovell], the mayor of Reading, England, was there and I remember wearing my First Communion suit," recalls Rick.

The escalator immediately attracted the attention of customers of all demographics, but the store regained its upper-crust image once the fascination diminished. Meiser comments, "If you wanted something higher in quality, you went to Whitner's, but they never had the selection or inventory that Pomeroy's had." In 1967, Whitner's installed a modernized storefront and began expansion plans. In August 1970, a smaller location opened in Reading's Berkshire Mall, followed by another satellite store at the Exton Square Mall in 1973. The lease agreement for the Berkshire Mall Whitner's was "ridiculous," and the Exton location was "too small and too far" from Reading. However, declining sales at the downtown store forced company officials and family members to make the difficult decision to close its main Penn Street store. In June 1981, after a bankruptcy filing, Whitner's closed its doors. On its final day of operation, one forty-year veteran employee told the *Reading Eagle*, "I don't think I ever cried so much in my life. It broke your heart." John Whitner Rick felt sympathy for his employees who had worked at the stores for years and years. "We had very good employees," states Rick. After many years of sitting vacant, the former downtown Whitner's was demolished in 2004 and replaced by the Sovereign Plaza.

On September 24, 1931, Read's Department Store began its tenure at Seventh and Penn Streets in downtown Reading. Described as "unquestionably the most beautiful department store structure in Reading," the firm advertised itself as "a new kind of department store." Owned and operated by Interstate Department Stores Inc., Read's was "Reading's Largest Cash Department Store." Department store historian David Sullivan cites the business as "one of Interstate's generic divisions that had the exciting name of 'Read's' because it was in Reading." Read's pledged to "sell no seconds, refund money any time, and do its best to save for you." It opened during the height of the Great Depression and targeted customers who shopped Pomeroy's Basement Store. However, by the end of 1958, Read's was just a memory.

Ellis Mills, "Reading's Dependable Store," came to town in 1910 by way of Pottstown. Located at 647–49 Penn Street in Reading, the Ellis Mills Store acquired the J. Mould & Company "Bee Hive" store. Mills enjoyed a "large patronage by fair dealing and intelligent application to business...but the depression came as a hard blow to the Reading."[69] The Reading store closed in June 1939 because of increased competition from Pomeroy's Bargain Basement and Read's, but the original Pottstown location continued for numerous decades.

In 1911, Solomon Boscov arrived in Reading with only $1.37 and a pair of shoes. A Russian immigrant, Boscov did not wear the shoes—he carried them. "Sol Boscov would tell you that he carried his shoes because anybody knew that if you walked the skin off of your feet it would grow back and become callouses, which were even better," stated an article in *Berksiana* magazine.[70] After peddling throughout Lancaster and Berks Counties, he opened Boscov's Economy Shoe and Dry Goods Store at Ninth and Pike Streets in the city of Reading. The store was located in the bottom floor of a rowhouse, and Solomon, along with his wife and three children, lived above and behind the business. It was a sharp contrast to Pomeroy's and Whitner's along Penn Street. Over the next several decades, this neighborhood business became America's largest independently run family department store, with a fiercely loyal staff and customer base along with a national reputation of innovation and success.

By the 1950s, Boscov had acquired the adjacent rowhouses along Ninth Street and transitioned from a shoe and dry goods store into Boscov's Department Store. Boscov placed a bell over the store's main entrance to signal a customer's arrival. As the store grew, these bells rang at "five and ten second intervals." When banker Sydney Klein noticed Boscov's Ninth Street success, he funded the company's first suburban expansion in Sinking Spring, called "Boscov's West." An immediate success, Boscov's continued its expansion and opened "Boscov's North" in 1965 at the Reading Fairgrounds and "Boscov's East" in Exeter Township in 1967.

On February 2, 1967, the original Boscov's store on Ninth Street was destroyed in a general alarm fire. The blaze erupted at about 2:30 p.m., and customers and employees fled the "massive flames." Al Boscov recalls, "The fire was shocking, not very nice, and it was an all-wood store." As the firm picked up the pieces at the old Ninth Street store, Boscov's concentrated on a new location, scheduled for a holiday season opening. But in a bizarre twist of fate, the company suffered another blow on November 20, 1967. On the very same day that Boscov's celebrated the grand opening of its Exeter Township "Boscov's East" store, a fire destroyed Boscov's West. The fire started in an incinerator and shocked Solomon; his son, Albert; and his son-in-law, Edwin Lakin, as they toured the rubble. "It's a heckuva loss because we're still small. The stores we own have become very personal. Two big fires like this in one year make you feel a little older," said Albert Boscov.[71]

The unfortunate events did not deter Boscov's expansions. The Ninth Street location never reopened, but Boscov's continued its march into the suburbs and other Pennsylvania cities. As Boscov's grew, Pomeroy's generally stayed still. Pomeroy's remained a downtown fixture, while suburban shopping centers, such as the Berkshire Mall, drew shoppers who wanted

The original Boscov's in Reading, Pennsylvania, at Ninth and Pike Streets, originally operated as Boscov's Department Store and Economy Shoe and Dry Goods store. *Courtesy of Boscov's Department Stores.*

Before the devastating fire in February 1967, the original Boscov's exterior was modernized. All of its adjoining buildings were covered with a uniform tin material. *Courtesy of Boscov's Department Stores.*

to shop closer to home. Boscov's never considered a downtown Reading store. "We saw what was going on in downtown Reading and [noticed that] the city population was dropping and the county population was growing," says Albert Boscov. In 1954, Albert Boscov and Edwin Lakin joined the management of the firm. After Solomon retired in 1968, they continued to lead the store's prosperity and popularity. Once considered a "pipsqueak store" by its own management, Boscov's became a major competitor to Pomeroy's; by the 1980s, it was the dominant store in Reading.

Chapter 8
5/5/55

After World War II, Americans enjoyed a period of prosperity that was driven by advanced employment opportunities combined with transportation changes. Suburban developments were perceived as new and clean, and many inner-city businesses and buildings were in need of renovations and greater parking availability. By the late 1940s, Allied Stores, Pomeroy's parent company, had begun exploring shopping opportunities located just outside of its major metropolitan markets. A 1947 Allied Stores Corporation study proved that suburban migration from "congested city centers" had begun in the 1920s and consistently grew in the 1930s. The march to the suburbs accelerated during the 1940s, and Allied Stores began to invest in one-stop regional shopping centers located within a fifteen-minute drive from its residential customer base. Allied Stores entered the 1950s with new branch stores such as Bon Marche–Northgate near Seattle, Jordan Marsh-Shoppers' World near Boston and Stern Brothers-Bergen Mall in Paramus, New Jersey.

In 1947, Allied formed the Alstores Realty Corporation. This subsidiary assisted the company with store building improvements and construction and major rehabilitation projects. Other Allied divisions—such as Gertz in Queens; Titche-Goettinger in Dallas; and Levy's in Savannah, Georgia—underwent significant modernizations to their downtown facilities that included necessities such as air conditioning and parking structures.[72] At this time, Pomeroy's chose to invest in upgrades to its inner-city Pennsylvania stores rather than the development of suburban branches.

The Levittown Pomeroy's store, as it appeared shortly after its 1955 opening. *Collection of the author.*

On December 8, 1950, L.S. Hubbard, managing director of the Reading Pomeroy's, flipped the switch to the store's new moving stairways. After three months of installation construction, the escalators linked the Reading store's first floor to its third floor. Santa Claus was the first rider on the new system, and crowds flocked to see him take the first ride.[73] It was not the first escalator in Reading. Whitner's had installed its escalators in 1948, but Pomeroy's was a bigger and busier store than Whitner's. "Kids would pay seven cents just to take the trolley downtown and ride Pomeroy's escalator," recalls George M. Meiser IX. "It was a great big deal. As kids, you were allowed to ride the escalators one or two times before they'd ask you to leave."

Pomeroy's employed a floorwalker to monitor the children and any activity within the store. Former employee Leonard Miller remembers one female floorwalker. "All the kids knew who the floorwalker was," says Miller. "She would hide behind counters, and she didn't trust anybody. She especially didn't like the Catholic kids. She thought that they were just bad kids." This floorwalker also kept a watchful eye on the store employees. Miller recalls,

"[While working in the display windows,] she would watch us as we selected merchandise within the store. Sometimes you would stick something in your pockets when your hands were full, but she would check your bags [as you were leaving work]." In addition to the moving stairways, Pomeroy's modernized its Sixth Street entrance and main sales floor within the next few years.

In 1955, Pomeroy's completed major renovations to its stores in Pottsville and Wilkes-Barre. The Pottsville renovation, completed in early 1955, included a new brick storefront that disguised its original appearance. The Wilkes-Barre store was much grander in size. In February 1954, Pomeroy's embarked on a $2 million modernization program that included a four-story addition, air conditioning and the installation of high-speed elevators. The plan increased the store's ninety thousand square feet of retail space by 50 percent. It was part of a three-stage renovation that involved a new storefront in the near future that would help "transform the store into one of the finest and most modern department stores in the country."[74]

After nearly eighteen months of construction work, Pomeroy's held a grand reopening of its Wilkes-Barre store on September 12, 1955. Vaughn Monroe, the "Voice of RCA Victor," entertained the crowds on the store's fourth-floor television center, and Julia Meade, hostess of the television program *Your Hit Parade*, autographed photographs in the first-floor cosmetic department. Mayor Luther Kniffen predicted that the renovation would bring "a growing and satisfied patronage, a situation which will be of mutual gratification to the public and the store," and gave his "best wishes for a lasting prosperity."[75] Allied Stores chairman and chief executive officer B. Earl Puckett was scheduled as one of the guests of honor at the celebration. Bettijane Long Eisenpreis, the wife of assistant managing director Alfred Eisenpreis, recalls that Puckett's arrival in Wilkes-Barre was not without problems:

Opposite, top: This 1940s image of the downtown Pottsville Pomeroy's shows a Frigidaire promotion in its main corner display window. Pomeroy's signage informed customers to "Live Better and Save Money" with Frigidaire electric ranges and refrigerators. *Courtesy of the Historical County of Schuylkill County.*

Opposite, bottom: The Pottsville Pomeroy's celebrates Pomeroy Days in addition to its modern, updated frontage. *Courtesy of the Historical County of Schuylkill County.*

[B. Earl Puckett] *was flying out to the grand opening, but it was foggy and the plane had trouble landing* [at the airport] *in Avoca. By the time he arrived at the store, the reception was about over. Earl asked Alfred to come up to his hotel room to talk. He told him to grab some booze and sandwiches. Well, Alfred needed ice, and he grabbed two buckets of ice but later realized that one of the buckets was contaminated from a recent flood. He realized that he did something horrible. Wilkes-Barre rolls up its sidewalks at 9:00 p.m., but Alfred finally found a diner and blew most of Pomeroy's budget to get the diner owner to sell him some ice!*

For the celebration, Pomeroy's adopted a new slogan, "Especially for You," that emphasized the new pleasant, easy and modern environment of the department store. The slogan supplemented the longtime advertising tagline that reminded residents to "Shop Pomeroy's First."

The same day that Pomeroy's celebrated its Wilkes-Barre groundbreaking in February 1954, the department store announced its plan for a new suburban location in Levittown, Pennsylvania. Designed by developer William J. Levitt, it capitalized on the success of Levittown, New York, and was Levitt's second planned community that embodied the American dream. Located in Lower Bucks County and just south of Trenton, Levittown's welcomed its first residents on June 23, 1952, and grew to 17,311 homes by 1957.[76] Levitt selected Pomeroy's to anchor the "largest and most diversified shopping center in the nation." Designed to anchor the new Shop-a-Rama, Pomeroy's was the largest department store between Philadelphia and Newark.[77] The new Levittown store was Pomeroy's fifth location and its first suburban shopping center operation.

Bill Levitt did not initially seek out Pomeroy's as an anchor store for his new shopping center. Former managing director Lee Starr states that Levitt, a "strong, dynamic, and egotistical man," approached the large Philadelphia retailers and gauged their interest. "Wanamaker's and Strawbridge & Clothier did not feel that [Levittown's] income level could support their kind of store," recalls Starr. However, Bill Levitt was attracted to Allied's early development of regional shopping centers, such as Northgate in Seattle and Shoppers' World in Framingham, Massachusetts. With Allied's support, Lee Starr secured the deal with Levitt. Once the deal was signed, Allied officials told Starr, "You recommended that we open this store, now do it."[78] Starr calls his early involvement at Levittown "a great experience for a young guy." He adds, "[Pomeroy's Levittown store] was a brand-new store in a brand-new community. We had to create a store from nothing!"

An undated birthday celebration at the downtown Wilkes-Barre Pomeroy's included dignitaries, a ribbon cutting and an American Legion drum and bugle corps. *Collection of the Luzerne County Historical Society.*

Lee D. Starr came to Levittown by way of the Bon Ton store in Lebanon, where he served as its managing director. Jack Matusek, a former buyer at the Levittown store, calls Lee Starr "the nicest person. I adored him. You can't say that about most of your top executives." Like Matusek, Starr moved into one of Levitt's new homes, along with his wife and children. "Lee came down from New York and bought a house without his wife seeing it," says Matusek. "We were able to afford a new house [in Levittown] with no money down. We assumed a former GI mortgage at 4 percent. I had a house with all of the modern conveniences, with schools, shopping centers, thirty minutes from Philadelphia, one hour from New York, two hours from the mountains, two hours from the Shore and paid only sixty-five to seventy dollars a month for the mortgage."

In November 1954, six months before its grand opening, Starr mailed out a survey to more than twenty thousand households, asking customers what they were looking for in the new store. The overwhelming demand was for

Tuesday Evening, December 21, 1954

POMEROY'S SANTA CLAUS
IS COMING TO LEVITTOWN ON
WEDNESDAY 1:00 P.M.
At The Baseball Field Beside The Administration Building

YES...Santa is coming To Levittown To Look at POMEROY'S New Store and to say HELLO to all his little Friends!!

SEE SANTA LAND IN HIS HELICOPTER!

SING CHRISTMAS CAROLS WITH SANTA

Before the store opened on May 5, 1955, Santa visited Levittown in December 1954 to "look at Pomeroy's new store and say hello to all his little friends." *Collection of the author.*

better merchandise that would "round out the already plentiful inexpensive items available at other nearby stores."[79] Other results included the need for a restaurant, delivery service, adequate restrooms and lounges, along with a community auditorium. Because these suggestions were already built into the store's planning, Starr was confident that the Levittown operation, built of Pennsylvania stone, was "heading in the right direction."

Pomeroy's Levittown store opened its doors on Thursday, May 5, 1955. It was a success from the very first day. "The Levittown store was really a community store," states Matusek. "It had real customer loyalty. If you shopped at Pomeroy's, you didn't go anywhere else. One woman

Pomeroy's new Levittown store exterior was featured on matchbooks that were distributed in the store's Bucks County Room restaurant. *Collection of Lois Witmer.*

A postcard of the Levittown Shop-a-Rama showed a landscaped walkway and the Pomeroy's store in the distance. *Collection of the author.*

[employee] burned a batch of chocolate chip cookies every morning 'just to make the aroma.'" Matusek also remembers the store closing for one day every summer for a company picnic. "They would place an ad that said, 'Gone Fishin.'" In its earlier years, the Levittown Pomeroy's hosted appearances by popular figures, from Captain Kangaroo to Mary Martin to Senator John F. Kennedy. The store's sales grew as the suburban community grew. "Whenever a new subdivision opened, we noticed the sales rise," notes former buyer Mike Carratilo. The Levittown store became very engaged with local community organizations as it built its customer base. "We had a Consumer Advisory Board that included the presidents of all of the area's women's clubs," recalls former managing director Lee Starr. "The board met once a month, and the members shared ideas and suggestions. One day, [Pomeroy's] turned the store over to club members, and they ran the store. Their clubs earned a percentage of the day's sales," notes Starr.

Originally managed by the Wilkes-Barre store, Pomeroy's Levittown eventually became its own operating division within Allied Stores. Allied Stores' corporate policy was based on good employee relations and strong executive training programs. "The Company maintains a very active interest in the welfare of the people who work for it, particularly in respect to the individual's opportunity for reasonable security, growth, and progress," stated a corporate report. Pomeroy's, with its five locations, was a member of Allied's "Group H," which included other Allied stores such as Mabley & Carew in Cincinnati; Dey Brothers in Syracuse; Wren's in Springfield, Ohio; and Troutman's of Greensburg, Pennsylvania. "We all became friends," says Matusek. "The group was very close-knit, like family, and there was a lot of bonding between employees." Matusek believes that this was due to the customer service practices observed by Group H. "People actually waited on you. We had salespeople in every department who performed all types of tasks. They sold merchandise and took care of the customers. People had a real loyalty to Pomeroy's."

In spite of its success, Pomeroy's did not open another suburban store for more than ten years, even as other department store chains from Philadelphia and other cities expanded beyond their downtown flagship bases. Before long, stores like John Wanamaker, Strawbridge & Clothier and Lit Brothers had entered Pomeroy's long-established sales territories. Although rich in customer loyalty, the company soon learned that it needed to grow in order to address increased urban and suburban competition.

Chapter 9

BEYOND THE CITY LIMITS

As the 1950s progressed, many department store companies were at a crossroads with their downtown operations. These retailers realized that their massive buildings were growing older and were in need of substantial upgrades and maintenance projects. However, even more important, America's inner-city residents were relocating to suburbia. The 1950s were not the easiest years for the Allied Stores Corporation, the parent of Pomeroy's. Prior to 1950, Allied was the "undisputed leader" in the department store industry in terms of size and sales. But in 1957, Allied lost the top spot to Federated Department Stores, which gained strength by investing heavily in suburban branch development.

Even though it enjoyed success at its suburban Levittown store, Pomeroy's turned its attention to renovating and updating its downtown buildings. In April 1959, Pomeroy's began a large-scale renovation at its downtown Harrisburg store. The plan included a "major rearrangement and redecoration of all departments." Two new features brought the most fanfare: electric stairs and air doors. On September 26, 1959, children were invited to come to the downtown Harrisburg Pomeroy's and be the first people to ride the electric stairs. A Trans World Airlines (TWA) captain and two TWA stewardesses were on hand "to instruct children on the important rules for riding the moving stairs."[80] After receiving the instruction, the children took their escalator ride and earned TWA Gold Pilot Wings and Silver Stewardess Wings.

On October 19, 1959, the store celebrated the installation of three new air doors along Fourth Street and Market Street. Also referred to as "doorless

doors," this addition gave customers the luxury of not having to open doors while holding packages. Customers entered the store by walking through a grated airway that blew air vertically and moderated the temperature between the interior and the exterior. "It was wonderful when they installed the air doors," says Lee Spitalny. "Everybody was so excited when it happened." Historian Ken Frew adds, "The air doors technically kept the insects out and the heat in."

Left: A Pomeroy's advertisement from September 1959 celebrates the installation of its electric stairs at the downtown Harrisburg store. A TWA captain and two stewardesses were on hand to instruct children on the important rules for riding the moving stairs. *Collection of the author.*

Opposite, top: In 1959, construction crews began to prepare the Wilkes-Barre store for its new ceramic tile exterior. Many of the building's signature architectural details, including its peaked roof, were removed as part of this process. *Collection of the Luzerne County Historical Society.*

Opposite, bottom: The downtown Wilkes-Barre Pomeroy's, located on the city's Public Square, is almost unrecognizable after its 1960 "updating." *Collection of the Luzerne County Historical Society.*

On October 29, 1959, Pomeroy's unveiled "a new look to usher in the second century" at its Wilkes-Barre store. Pomeroy's transformed its signature mid-Victorian brick building on Public Square into a "clean, clear-lined structure" covered in ceramic turquoise tile, highlighted by aluminum grillwork.[81] Designed by Lacy, Atherton & Davis and constructed by the Sordoni Construction Company, the new storefront was hailed by city officials as "one of the most modern in the country." These officials felt that Pomeroy's renovation was "indicative of the faith the downtown businesses have in the future of Wilkes-Barre as the center for area-wide business."[82] Although its tall peaked roof, striking main archway and exterior decorative detail were all removed, Wilkes-Barre celebrated the building's new appearance as a sign of progress. "The building had a 'retro' appearance to it," says John Maday. "When you looked at it, you just accepted it." The new storefront was the culmination of a three-step renovation program that started in 1954. It coincided with the 100th anniversary of the business that initially began as the Jonas Long's Sons store in 1860.

A modernization plan was also put into place in downtown Reading. In addition to a new air-conditioning system, the Reading store received its own exterior renovation. In 1960, a modern ceramic tile and granite storefront was installed on the lower two floors of the building. Designed by architect Frederick A. Muhlenberg, the $500,000 remodeling project continued into 1962. Ceramic tile and granite were used to cover the façade from the sidewalk to the third floor along the Penn Street side of the building. The new design removed the mezzanine and second-floor windows, which required significant interior reconstruction. New vestibules with ceramic tile walls and slip-proof tile floors were installed. In addition, a new "third floor of fashion" was designed to upgrade the company's image. Morton M. Silton, the store's managing director, said, "This new improvement was just one more step on Pomeroy's part to stimulate the entire downtown Reading redevelopment program."[83]

Opposite, top: One of the busiest intersections in downtown Reading was located at Sixth and Penn Streets, home to Pomeroy's. This photograph was taken sometime after 1962, when the lower floors of the Reading building were covered with tile and granite. *Courtesy of the Historical Society of Berks County.*

Opposite, bottom: Shoppers hurriedly cross Reading's Sixth Street during the 1964 Christmas season. Pomeroy's famous Christmas windows are faintly visible in the photograph. *Courtesy of the Historical Society of Berks County.*

Behind the scenes, the company was working to revitalize the store's sagging sales. Downtown Reading began an era of decline that included "increased competition from new off-price retailers, including outlet stores, and shrinking property values." In spite of the national trend of suburban branch development, Pomeroy's remained committed to its inner-city Pennsylvania stores, with the exception of its lone suburban location in Levittown. However, by the early 1960s, Allied's suburban branch stores composed 60 percent of the company's sales, up from 25 percent ten years earlier.[84]

In 1913, Pomeroy's was one of the first store organizations to establish a sales and executive training program. As Pomeroy's became a unit of the Allied Stores Corporation, it adopted the procedures of the corporation's Executive Training and Development Program. As "a flexible program of continuous training and experience," it was designed to "prepare the executive for higher positions of greater responsibility in his special field." By the 1960s, the Executive Training and Development Program was open to women as well as men and sought people who were willing to "go as far up the ladder as your abilities will take you [and] Pomeroy's will train you every step of the way."[85] Regular classroom sessions covered such topics as merchandising policies and practices, store character, human relations and supervisory techniques. "When I graduated from the executive training program, Allied took all the graduates for a ride in its private plane," says Pat Eichorn. "We came from poor families and we were so in awe."

The Pomeroy's Builders' Club acted as an extension of the executive training program. The club membership included young executives who selected a yearlong topic that involved the investigation and study of a merchandising issue. The club gave "the up-and-coming young merchandisers an opportunity to express themselves and expound ideas of interest in the industry."[86] The executive training program was successful and developed a strong bond of loyalty among executives, employees and customers. According to Wilkes-Barre historian Tom Mooney, Pomeroy's and other large retailers were proud of their long-term workforce. "Pomeroy's [and the Boston Store] stressed careerism for their employees, though I also know that they employed a lot of part-time workers during the holidays. The newspapers often ran photos of workers being honored for forty or fifty years of service," said Mooney. "The managers of these stores were public figures, often pictured in the papers as helping with charity drives and other public events."

Pennsylvania experienced many of the same social changes that affected other American states. Numerous Pennsylvania cities witnessed a dramatic

In addition to its Executive Training Program and Builders' Club leadership group, Pomeroy's held employee enrichment classes at its Reading and Harrisburg stores. *Collection of Leonard Miller.*

flight of white residents from the city core. Racial tension was not limited to America's southern cities, and many large retailers did not offer welcoming environments to all customers. Lee Spitalny, wife of former Harrisburg manager Howard Spitalny, recalls one incident in the store's Tea Room. "One of Pomeroy's buyers was African American, and one day, he and I, along with my four-year-old child went to the Tea Room for lunch," says Spitalny. "Every eye [in the Tea Room] looked at my child thinking that it was 'our' child. I felt so uncomfortable for him."

Racial tension was not confined to Pennsylvania's inner cities. William Levitt, the builder of Levittown, home of Pomeroy's first suburban store, refused to sell homes to African Americans. In August 1957, an African American family moved into a residence at Daffodil and Deepgreen Lanes and was met with violent protests. The community of Levittown was divided between residents who supported equal rights and others who feared

Lebanon's Bon Ton predated Pomeroy's as a member of the Hahn Department Stores group. However by 1960, Allied Stores had begun to integrate Bon Ton into the Pomeroy's Harrisburg division. Bon Ton in Lebanon officially became a Pomeroy's store in September 1963. This advertisement from November 1960 reminds customers to "Shop the Bon Ton First." *Collection of the author.*

violence, forced integration and the possibility of intermarriage.[87] Pomeroy's Levittown auditorium was a frequent site for community meetings and forums that discussed these sensitive matters.

In addition to social changes, the country experienced international tensions, from the Cold War to Vietnam. Author Florence Ditlow notes, "Everything changed when Kennedy died. That's when people stopped wearing gloves and started wearing pants." Her comment references a rebellion toward established, formal traditions. Reading display employee Leonard Miller remembers Kennedy's death and its effect on the 1963 holiday season. "We had all of the windows filled with truckloads and truckloads of toys and life-sized Santas. But after he was killed, we removed every toy and draped every window in black. An easel holding Kennedy's picture and an American flag was placed in every window."

Despite the growth of the country's suburbs and its interstate highway system, Pomeroy's—and its parent company, Allied Stores Corporation—continued its commitment to center-city shopping. On Thursday, September 11, 1963, Pomeroy's opened its Lebanon, Pennsylvania branch store at Ninth and Cumberland Streets. The Pomeroy's store formerly operated as the Bon Ton, another Allied Stores division. Founded in 1896 by Louis Samler, Lebanon's Bon Ton store did not have a direct operating relationship with the larger Bon-Ton store maintained by S. Grumbacher & Son of York, Pennsylvania. According to an article in the *Lebanon Daily News*, Louis Samler married Samuel Grumbacher's daughter, Sophia. Sophia Grumbacher Samler was a shrewd businesswoman, and her business acumen was instrumental in the success of Lebanon's Bon Ton. Although the two stores shared the same name, they operated independently of each other. Originally referred to as the "Shirtwaist Store of Lebanon," it grew from a one-room operation into a forty-five-thousand-square-foot business with 110 employees.[88] The Bon Ton was one of the earliest members of Hahn Department Stores, the forerunner to the Allied Stores Corporation, becoming part of Hahn in 1933. The Bon Ton had its own holiday traditions, which included a Christmas parade and a visit from Santa Claus. "Santa landed [from an airplane] in a field in the eastern side of Lebanon and was taken by sled to downtown," recalls former store manager Anthony Kutchever. "The sled was brought up to Bon Ton, where Santa climbed a fire ladder to a second-floor window."

Lebanon's Bon Ton operation was one of Allied Stores' most profitable operations. Much of its success was due to the leadership of Albert Coons Sr. Coons was a distant relative of Louis Samler and was brought into Bon

For more than two decades, Pomeroy's operated the former Bon Ton store in Lebanon, Pennsylvania. *Collection of Lois Witmer.*

Ton's management because "Samler didn't want to do the work."[89] Coons was a shrewd businessman and built Bon Ton's business volume and catered to its unique customer base. Lee Starr feels that he learned much about the retail business from Albert Coons Sr. As the two men traveled throughout the state and visited the different stores in the Pennsylvania group, Albert Coons would tell Starr to turn the car off once he reached the top of a hill. "He would want the car to coast down the hill," says Starr. "He wanted to teach me a lesson on frugality." Some of the Bon Ton's best customers were from the area's Pennsylvania Dutch community. "On Friday nights, the farmers would come to town and pay cash for everything," states former Bon Ton managing director Lee Starr. "The store didn't even have an elevator, but the [Pennsylvania Dutch] would just carry any of the merchandise, large and small, down the stairs and out the doors."

Lebanon's proximity to Harrisburg and solid profitable operations made the Bon Ton store a good merger opportunity for the Harrisburg Pomeroy's operation. Former Lebanon store manager Anthony Kutchever remembers Bon Ton as "a little lower-priced store [than Pomeroy's], but once it became Pomeroy's, it adopted the qualities from Harrisburg." On its opening day in 1963, thousands of local residents lined up to see the new Pomeroy's. The first one thousand women to arrive received a free rose; the supply of roses was depleted within thirty-five minutes.[90] City officials hailed the $1 million renovation and stated, "This occasion represents a significant contribution to the progress of downtown Lebanon and reflects the confidence of Pomeroy's Inc. in the central business district." Pomeroy officials such as store president Harold Buchter; Allied vice-president Albert Coons Sr.; and his son, Albert Jr., senior merchandising manager, along with a member of the Samler family, helped cut the ribbon at the Lebanon location.

Allied wanted to replicate the success at the former Bon Ton in Lebanon with its Laubach's store in Easton, Pennsylvania. On August 1, 1964, the executive staff of Pomeroy's Reading store assumed control of William Laubach & Sons. Company officials stated that the two stores "have had a close working relationship for 15 years," and the merger was "designed to strengthen and improve the merchandising and customer service in both the Reading and Easton stores."[91] Founded in 1860, William Laubach & Sons opened his signature "Trade Palace" in 1872. In 1893, a ten-foot-tall replica of the newly invented Ferris wheel, featured at the Chicago World's Fair, was installed in Laubach's display windows. Shortly after its installation, the Ferris wheel caught fire, and the store was heavily damaged. But that setback did not prevent Laubach's from becoming Easton's largest and

In August 1964, Pomeroy's assumed the management of Easton's Laubach's store, a unit of the Allied Stores Corporation since 1947. The Easton branch never achieved its anticipated sales goals. *Collection of Lois Witmer.*

grandest store. Barbara Laubach Lehr contributed to an *Easton Express-Times* newspaper article about her family's store:

> *A sweeping staircase ascended from the main floor to the mezzanine and [it] must have looked like a stairway to heaven to the little ones who climbed it. The basement was a child's dream—a toy department that at Christmastime featured model trains that steamed and whistled like the real railroads that made Easton a hub. On the second floor, elegant hats occupied a space next to the beauty salon, where the smell of permanent wave lotion filled the air.*[92]

Jane Moyer, chief librarian at the Northampton Historical Society, recalls the heyday of the Easton landmark. "Laubach's was a family store and was well known for its hats, fine china and piece goods," says Moyer. "The store just made you feel special."

Allied Stores acquired Laubach's in 1947. Allied later converted Laubach's to the Pomeroy banner in order to reduce operating and managerial costs and stem sales declines. Many employees from the Reading store assisted the Easton store with its managing duties. "We used to go to Easton every other week to do the windows," says Reading display employee Leonard Miller. Carol Brightbill, of the Harrisburg store, recalls "going to Easton and visiting the departments and seeing how the stock was being represented and how the store was. This was before computers, and it's amazing how we did what we did."

Tomorrow 10 a.m.

POMEROY'S Burlington County

Opens it's doors!

Yes, tomorrow's the day — the day a big, beautiful new Pomeroy's opens its doors in Burlington County. Many of you are old friends. To many more of you shopping at Pomeroy's will be a new and, we're sure, pleasant experience. Pomeroy's offers you the first in fashions for your family and your home, the finest brands in the land — and courteous, competent service. Most of all, we believe you'll learn to depend on Pomeroy's for shopping satisfaction — guaranteed!

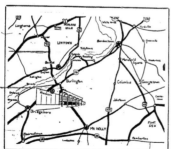

Opening day Program

Flag-raising ceremony at 9:45 A.M. you're invited to watch the brief opening ceremonies, with Willingboro Township officials, while Pomeroy's accepts an American flag from the Willingboro VFW Post 1149, and raises its own flag to signal the opening of the doors.

Miss Burlington County will be present at the opening and thereafter, to greet you

lovely models will show the latest fashions informally throughout the day

charming hostesses will be stationed at each entrance to direct you

radio station WBUD of Trenton will broadcast from its mobile trailer-station all day long - stop in and see it in action! And station WJJZ will be on hand to tape your reactions to this great new store, for broadcast over the weekend!

credit desks will be set up at convenient locations, so that you may have your credit application approved and shop as quickly as possible.

plus special demonstrations, trunk shows, excitement all day long!

shop 10 a.m. till 9 p.m. . . . Willingboro Plaza, Rte. 130, Willingboro, N. J.

Pomeroy's first "out of state" branch was in Willingboro, New Jersey, otherwise known as "Levittown, New Jersey." The large one-level Willingboro Plaza location opened on August 12, 1965. *Collection of the author.*

However, a number of Laubach's shoppers were not pleased with the changeover to Pomeroy's. "Laubach's was a far more superior store to Pomeroy's," notes Jane Moyer. "When Pomeroy's arrived, all of the old people were gone, and it was filled with cheaper merchandise. I never liked it. It wasn't a quality store. People in Easton noticed the change, but what are you going to do. It felt like a chain store." Pomeroy's was a relatively unknown name in the Easton area, and the transition altered Laubach's identity, and quality of merchandise and services. A number of former customers traveled to Hess Brothers in Allentown to fill the void created by the switchover.

After the Lebanon and Easton acquisitions, Pomeroy's once again turned its attention to suburban development. After building successful communities in New York and Pennsylvania, William Levitt began work on Levittown, New Jersey, in Burlington County. Levitt sold his first Levittown, New Jersey home in 1958, but the community was not the raging success of his other two large "towns." By the time it opened, Levittown, New Jersey, had experienced a softened postwar housing demand combined with an economic recession. Although more than fifteen thousand homes were planned for Levittown, New Jersey, only twelve thousand were constructed.[93] A 1959 referendum officially adopted the name "Levittown" for its unincorporated township.

Also in 1959, the first phase of a large shopping center, the Levittown Plaza, opened for business. It included an F.W. Woolworth, Food Fair and Penn Fruit Supermarkets. By 1963, the same residents who had approved the name Levittown for their township decided to return to the original name, Wellingborough, New Jersey (or "Willingboro"), for the immediate area. The Levittown Plaza followed suit and became the Willingboro Plaza. Its second phase added a Sears store in 1964. On August 12, 1965, Pomeroy's joined the Plaza during its third phase of construction. Pomeroy's Willingboro, New Jersey, was the company's first venture outside the Keystone State. The Willingboro store featured more than 110 departments, a "Villager Shop" for casual wear, a "Four Seasons sportswear shop," a "Trend Shop" for young men, a bridal shop with consultant and the Burlington Room restaurant.[94] Willingboro Plaza was located only about twenty minutes from the Levittown Shop-a-Rama, and the two Pomeroy's had a close working relationship. The one-story 175,000-square-foot store contrasted with the two-story 241,000-square-foot Levittown store. Former buyer Jack Matusek recalls, "[Willingboro] was developing thanks to the McGuire Air Force Base and Fort Dix. But we did around 20 percent less business at Willingboro than at Levittown. It was a 'better' department store and was perhaps too good for the area."

The quiet courtyard entrance to the Willingboro Pomeroy's, as seen in the mid-1980s. *Photograph by the author.*

Suburban expansion continued as the company opened a branch store at the new Midway Shopping Center, located between Wilkes-Barre and Scranton. Plans for the Midway location were announced in July 1965 and called for a thirty-thousand-square-foot department store and a ten-thousand-square-foot "automobile accessory center." The Midway store quickly doubled in size soon after its spring 1966 grand opening. William Dennis, managing director of the Wilkes-Barre store, stated that the new Midway store "testified to the faith that Pomeroy's has in Wyoming Valley and its tremendous economic growth potential."[95]

By the 1960s, the Allied Stores Corporation had chartered a new operational plan that combined suburban growth with productivity and profitability programs at its downtown stores.[96] In September 1965, the Reading, Pennsylvania Planning Commission recommended the construction of a two-block-long, seventy-foot-wide mall in the middle of Penn Square. The original plan called for a "closed mall on Penn Street from 6th to 8th and over a portion of 7th Street between Court and Franklin."[97] It was developed by Leonidas G. Vastardis. Penn Street faced constant logistical struggles, including the Seventh Street railroad tracks that interfered with the mall's

design. "We had a railroad that went right through the center of town!" says Reading display employee Leonard Miller. "On some nights, downtown would be so crowded, and then a train would come through. There would be hundreds of people waiting just to get across the tracks!"

Officials from the Downtown Reading Development Corporation debated a change to a vertical design, but the additional cost could not be "justified." Pomeroy's downtown Reading store was a crucial component of the new inner-city shopping mall, and the store agreed to its inclusion. The mall's success hinged on the addition of a second department store. As Penn Mall faced harsh criticism and stagnant progress, the new Berkshire Mall, in suburban Wyomissing, began construction in late 1968. The $25 million enclosed shopping mall included Philadelphia's John Wanamaker and Lit Brothers department stores. Because of its proximity to downtown, Pomeroy's opted to not pursue a location at the Berkshire Mall. It remained openly faithful to the downtown store and supported the proposed Penn Mall project.

Lois Witmer, a longtime employee in Harrisburg, says that Pomeroy's "was remodeled periodically and updated with the latest merchandise frequently and profits soared throughout the years." By the end of the 1960s, Allied's downtown stores totaled "only" 12.5 million square feet of space of the company's 27 million square feet of space.[98] One of the company's most successful stores opened in October 1968. Pomeroy's established its first Harrisburg-area suburban store in Camp Hill, on the city's West Shore. Pomeroy's chose Camp Hill "because the West Shore is the fastest-growing area in Greater Harrisburg—population-wise, industrially, and in service organization headquarters. For too many years, Pomeroy's Downtown [Harrisburg] store has been too small for the volume of sales it produces; business is good and is continually growing, but we can't enlarge here."[99] The company insisted that the sales per square foot in downtown Harrisburg were "considerably above the national average." Located on a triangular plot of land at Route 15 and Simpson Ferry Road, Pomeroy's Camp Hill contained two selling floors, an outdoor patio shop, a beauty salon and the self-service Fife 'n' Drum Buffeteria. The company proclaimed that it offered

Opposite, top: One of Pomeroy's most successful suburban operations was located in Camp Hill, just a few miles west of downtown Harrisburg. The Camp Hill store far exceeded the company's anticipated sales expectations. *Courtesy of the Bon-Ton Stores Inc.*

Opposite, bottom: These interior scenes, as printed in a corporate report, can most likely be attributed to the new Camp Hill store. *Collection of Lois Witmer.*

merchandise in all ranges and prices, from the more upscale Pacesetter and Villager shops to the Budget Center that featured quality, brand-name merchandise at modest price points.

Allied Stores anticipated an initial 25 percent sales drop at the downtown store as customers chose to spend their dollars at the new Camp Hill location, only four miles from Harrisburg's city center. Pomeroy's was not prepared for the rousing success of the branch—the flagship store's loss was actually much more. Employee Mary Custer recalls, "Camp Hill was on a lot all by itself. People felt that it wasn't going to have strong business with nothing else to draw in the customer." Buyer Pat Eichorn remembers, "The company was so nervous about the Camp Hill store because it stood alone." Former buyer Carol Brightbill adds, "The buyers [in Camp Hill] didn't have a lot of direction. We initially planned on achieving about one-half of the business at the downtown store. But we didn't stock enough merchandise [at first]. We were excited to see our shelves become bare at Camp Hill. It was wonderful!"

Even though it enjoyed immediate popularity, Pomeroy's Camp Hill had to overcome some challenges. "Camp Hill was planned to be attached to a mall that was never built," states former manager Ross Ricketts. "We always tried to find ways where we could do more for the customers. We tried to be very service-oriented as we developed our customer base. We organized an advisory board that met for lunch once a month to find out what they needed or liked. We developed a great relation with women [at Camp Hill]."

The downtown Reading Pomeroy's received many upgrades to its physical plant in the late 1960s. In addition to significant changes to its massive heating system and new high-speed passenger elevators, Pomeroy's completely remodeled its main floor in 1968 and its second floor in 1969. These renovations were followed by a modernization of the basement floor, designed to "give the people of Berks County the finest department store facilities and merchandise available under the oldest established and accepted name of Pomeroy's."[100]

Another addition to the Reading store was the reappearance of the bronze sculpture *Boy with Mandolin*, which was placed in an alcove outside the Tea Room. The five-hundred-pound, four-and-a-half-foot-tall statue was purchased by George S. Pomeroy during the 1920s. Former manager Ross Ricketts discovered the sculpture, by Ephraim Keyser, in a dusty corner of a seventh-floor storage space. Ricketts lugged it to the lobby outside the basement Tea Room sometime in the late 1960s. The statue was a very visible meeting point for Tea Room customers. Barbara Korczykowski, granddaughter of George S. Pomeroy Jr., recalls the sculpture and said, "I thought it was huge, but I also thought it was ugly. You couldn't miss it. I guess I wasn't into art."

Pomeroy's downtown Reading store faced increased competition from the new Berkshire Mall, as well as the new Vanity Fair Factory Outlet. Opened in 1970, the VF Factory Outlet was the first outlet center in the country and grew from a small store in the "largest full-fashioned hosiery mill in the world" into a fifty-store shopping complex spread throughout eight buildings. The outlet was located just a few minutes west of downtown Reading and changed the face of retail in Reading. Former Whitner's chairman John Whitner Rick explains how the new mall and outlet complex affected traditional retailers: "People started going to the malls, where they could park for free. If people couldn't find what they wanted at the mall, they'd go to the outlets. But the outlets were about price, not quality. Our store had quality. Our downtown customers had to deal with increasing bus fare. It was awful."

Two new suburban stores were announced in 1971. The company reported the construction of a 181,000-square-foot branch at the Concord Mall in Delaware, about six miles north of downtown Wilmington. After a successful 1966 opening, Concord Mall management wanted to expand, and the shopping complex needed a second anchor department store to complement Almart, another Allied store.[101] The addition of Pomeroy's created Delaware's largest shopping center, and the mall expansion was scheduled for a summer 1972 completion.[102] The Concord Mall location became the company's second and final out-of-Pennsylvania store. Fashion director Dorothy Mugford says, "Concord was the big store. They had everything that the others didn't. They had the big-ticket merchandise." Buyer Mike Carratilo agrees: "Wilmington set the retail standard. It was the second-best chain-wide store behind Camp Hill." Former managing director Anthony Kutchever cites Concord's success "because it was basically merchandised like the [most upscale] Harrisburg stores."

The other important suburban store was located at the Wyoming Valley Mall in Wilkes-Barre. The 159,000-square-foot Wyoming Valley Mall store opened in 1971 and was Pomeroy's third operation in the Wilkes-Barre market. Many local residents had grown accustomed to downtown shopping, but the Pomeroy's on Public Square became an aging, "run-down and rough plant."[103] The Boston Store was the biggest and busiest store in Wilkes-Barre. Shoppers were initially reluctant to change their shopping habits, but "once the Wyoming Valley Mall store finally got off of the ground, it took over the town," recalls former managing director Lee Starr. By June of the following year, the Wyoming Valley store had assumed an even more important role in the community and eventually became the second-highest-grossing location in the entire corporation.

Chapter 10

WHILE SUPPLIES LAST

On June 22, 1972, the remains of Hurricane Agnes moved over Pennsylvania and inundated the state with almost 14 trillion gallons of water.[104] With forty-eight reported deaths and $2.1 billion in damage, it was Pennsylvania's worst natural disaster. Its anticipated severity was underestimated, and the storm lingered for days, heavily affecting all of Pomeroy's trading areas. Cities like Reading and Pottsville suffered as the Schuylkill River overran its banks and crippled water, sewer, gas and electrical systems. In Harrisburg, Governor Milton Shapp and his wife, Muriel, were rescued by boat from the governor's mansion. The worst damage and devastation centered on Wilkes-Barre.

The city of Harrisburg was devastated as the Susquehanna River rose fifteen feet above flood stage. Water deluged the city's residential and business districts. The flooding closed downtown businesses, and hundreds of National Guardsmen arrived to control the city. More than 15 percent of Harrisburg was under water, and the city suffered damage totaling more than $100 million. Pomeroy's advertised that it would reopen as soon as electrical power was restored to the city center. "I don't think that the water got into the store," recalls former employee Lois Witmer. "Many employees weren't able to cross the Susquehanna River, but after about four days, we were called back to work." The situation in the capital was dire, but "by Saturday morning [June 24], Harrisburg began to lose its dubious distinction of being the hardest-hit area of the state."

On June 23, the Susquehanna rose eighteen feet above flood stage in Wilkes-Barre and crested at nearly forty-one feet. Area residents frantically

After the historic flooding from Tropical Storm Agnes, many areas of Wilkes-Barre, including the community's Public Square, were devastated by the floodwaters. A number of prominent downtown businesses, such as Pomeroy's, were closed for many months, while others, such as the Isaac Long Store located next to the S.S. Kresge store, were never rebuilt. *Courtesy of John J. Rygiel.*

filled sandbags and worked to fight the rising waters. Wilkes-Barre was protected by an extensive levee system, but it was no match for Hurricane Agnes's floodwaters. Water surged into the city and filled downtown businesses up to their doorways and first-floor ceilings. On Public Square, home to Pomeroy's downtown store, no store window survived intact.[105] Some Pomeroy's employees had been called in to prepare the store for probable floodwaters. Buyer Mike Carratilo recalls, "We moved all of the merchandise from the basement and first floor to the second floor. But we left the elevator in the basement instead of the fifth floor. The whole system was flooded out."

The suburban Midway Shopping Center Pomeroy's experienced extensive damage. Located near the Forty Fort Cemetery, the shopping center was submerged within twenty minutes as a dike collapsed near the cemetery. The force of the water unearthed caskets at the cemetery.[106] "We got a call [at the Levittown store] after the flood and went to Wilkes-Barre to help," says buyer Jack Matusek. "The Midway store was just wiped out by the flood. There were caskets in the store that crashed in through the store windows."

While the downtown and Midway stores were temporarily shuttered, the Wyoming Valley Mall cashed in. "The Wyoming Valley store was the only store that survived," says Ross Ricketts. "I remember people coming into Pomeroy's with government passes that were issued to purchase new goods. People would just try on the clothes, use their passes and leave wearing new clothes." Even though the basement and first floor of the downtown Wilkes-Barre store were submerged, workers were able to take clothing from the store's second floor and move it to the Wyoming Valley Mall location. "We also brought in special orders of ironing boards and mops," says Ricketts. Mike Carratilo states, "Customers needed the basics—T-shirts, underwear, panty hose. We kept on ordering and ordering, and the merchandise kept going out quicker and quicker." Personnel director June Bonning agrees: "After the flood, the Wyoming Valley store finally got off the ground." Chamber of Commerce employee John Maday adds, "The mall struggled until the flood. [Afterward] it became the only game in town. People needed to buy stuff, and that is how the mall became successful." As the demand for goods grew, the government relaxed its Blue Laws so that flood survivors could have the option of Sunday shopping to help rebuild their lives.

Many businesses never returned to downtown Wilkes-Barre. Isaac Long's, a division of John Wanamaker's and Pomeroy's Public Square neighbor, never reopened after the flood. However, by the end of 1972, a number of the damaged stores had resurrected. When downtown Pomeroy's finally reopened, it struggled to maintain its sales force. "The downtown store had trouble with employment after the flood," states Bonning. "Employees were coming and going, trying to get their lives together. Pomeroy's was able to recover and reestablish the downtown store." Damage from Hurricane Agnes required post-flood reconstruction of the area, which in turn merged with a federal urban redevelopment program that had begun even before the flood. The result was a large-scale demolition and rebuilding of downtown Wilkes-Barre.

In early 1973, Pomeroy's began construction of its second suburban Harrisburg store. Located at the Colonial Park Mall, the 137,000-square-foot branch store was built to serve the city's East Side residents. When its doors opened on July 25, 1974, Pomeroy's invited area children to "immortalize themselves" by imprinting their hands in cement in celebration of the new store. The downtown, Camp Hill and Colonial Park stores, when combined, provided 462,000 square feet of retailing space for Harrisburg shoppers. The three Harrisburg stores ended up serving three separate markets. "Colonial Park was a good store, but it didn't do the volume of Camp Hill," states buyer Carol Brightbill. "I think there might have been more competition on the East Side." Former Camp Hill manager Ross Ricketts notes that Camp

Public Square in Wilkes-Barre struggled to recover after Tropical Storm Agnes, as seen during this Christmas 1974 photograph. This construction site was the former location of the destroyed Isaac Long department store. *Collection of the Luzerne County Historical Society.*

Hill had a higher income base than the East Side. "Very few people would travel from Camp Hill to Colonial Park," says Ricketts.

However, the retailing scene deteriorated in downtown Harrisburg. By the end of the 1970s, Bowman's and Sears had closed their downtown stores and left Pomeroy's as the city's sole anchor store. "Downtown was getting sad," says Brightbill. "We used to have a big lunch crowd, but businesses like Bell Telephone [eventually] slimmed down." Pomeroy's soon dropped its annual Christmas window displays, a holiday tradition for Harrisburgers. "I don't know why they stopped the windows," states thirty-two-year veteran employee Lois Witmer. "It was a big mistake. It was such a great reason to come downtown and shop."

The downtown customer base evolved into a lunch hour trade during workdays, as well as less affluent shoppers who relied on public transportation. The *Patriot-News* bemoaned the evolution of Harrisburg's downtown:

Before suburban malls and strip stores came on the scene, the downtown, with its major department stores, 5- and 10-cent stores, drug stores, sporting goods stores, book stores, jewelry stores, shoe stores and candy shops, was a destination for young and old at Christmas or, for that matter, any time of the year... Department stores were special with their multiple floors, bargain basements, elevators operated by a person who sat on a little jump seat ("Floors, please"), escalators, cash registers at each department or a pneumatic tube cash conveyor and signature shopping bags, hat boxes and gift boxes.[107]

With its high ceilings, escalators and elevators, "Pomeroy's was the only place in Reading that had that big-city experience," says David Korczykowski. "You went downtown when you really needed something. There was a great presentation [of the merchandise] along with sales people that were there to help you." But David Korczykowski admits that this was before the suburbs blossomed with single-family homes, business and entertainment options that offered late hours and free parking, as well as new out-of-town retailers with competitive prices and wide selections. His wife, Barbara, great-granddaughter of George S. Pomeroy Sr., fondly remembers the large red Pomeroy's rooftop sign as she drove across the Penn Street Bridge, but she was aware of the changes and challenges that faced downtown Reading. "Everything started to change in the 1970s," said Barbara Korczykowski. "The city was taking on a different flair."

However, Pomeroy's biggest breakthrough in Reading occurred when the Berkshire Mall Lit Brothers space opened up just before Christmas 1975. Pomeroy's management stressed that the company was committed to its downtown Reading store even though it was located only two miles from the Berkshire Mall. "We're going to try to service two markets," said managing director Joseph R. Colarusso. "There is a good suburban market and a good downtown market [in Reading]. We've got a lot of money in this [downtown] building. We have a large financial commitment to downtown Reading and we aren't going to give it up."[108]

The move into the Berkshire Mall was a complicated one for Pomeroy's and Allied Stores. "When we bought Lit Brothers at the Berkshire Mall, Lits only produced $3 million in annual sales," says Allied executive Lee Starr. "But we still had to send people down to Washington and help alleviate anti-trust issues and convince leaders that we were still committed to the downtown Reading store for a certain amount of years." Joseph Colarusso was frustrated that the proposed Penn Mall project, once dubbed "the savior of the downtown business district," was abandoned in 1975. "Very obviously

This rare collage of photographs shows six of the central Pennsylvania Pomeroy's locations. *Clockwise from the top*: Downtown Harrisburg, Berkshire Mall (Reading), Camp Hill (Harrisburg), Downtown Reading, Colonial Park (Harrisburg) and Downtown Lebanon. *Collection of Lois Witmer.*

we would have preferred it to happen," states Colarusso. Former employee Shirley Becker remembers, "When Pomeroy's opened at Berkshire [on May 5, 1976], they asked a few of us if we would transfer. It was a hard decision. I loved working downtown, but the mall was only five minutes from home." In response to the success at Berkshire Mall, former Reading manager Ross Ricketts approached the Allied Stores corporate office to propose substantial renovation to the downtown store. "I was told [by Allied], 'If I gave you $10 million, would it be better spent on redoing the downtown store or building another mall store?' I agreed that if we didn't have the new Berkshire Mall store, business at Pomeroy's would have been tough."

Reading was not alone in urban retail challenges. The aging downtown Easton location closed its doors on December 24, 1976, due to declining sales and sat vacant for decades. "The Easton store never really fit into Pomeroy's," says former managing director Lee Starr. "Albert Coons only bought it [in 1947] because it was available." Former manager Ross Ricketts recalls, "I helped move the unsold merchandise of the Easton store to the Reading Basement store once it closed." Even with its fiercely loyal suburban audience, the Levittown Pomeroy's experienced its own set of challenges as competition intensified around the community. Former Levittown buyer John Matusek recalls, "In the 1970s, there was a proliferation of stores [near Levittown], which made it too hard to split the pie. They were building shopping centers like gas stations, one on every corner." Unlike the Levittown Shop-a-Rama, large area enclosed malls (such as Neshaminy Mall and Oxford Valley Mall) were designed by professional shopping center developers. These malls became retail destinations, while the Levittown Shop-a-Rama catered to its local, immediate market.

Philadelphia department stores infiltrated the Reading, Harrisburg and Levittown markets. Levittown buyer Mike Carratilo says that Pomeroy's "was so busy trying to keep up with the competition from the Philadelphia stores. Pomeroy's became the small fish in a very large pond." Carratilo remembers one store meeting when a former Pomeroy's managing director used the phrase, "Put the slop down where the hogs can get at it! [In other words] if you have something that sells, buy it, pile it deep and shove it in their face!" Pomeroy's success was geared to the moderate customer, emphasizing necessities over luxuries. "There was one buyer at the Levittown store who said that her best customers were 'Polly' and 'Esther,'" says Harrisburg buyer Carol Brightbill.

Strawbridge & Clothier, John Wanamaker and Bamberger's encroached on Pomeroy's territory and offered higher-end merchandise to the Bucks County market. Carratilo thinks that Strawbridge & Clothier, through its Neshaminy Mall store, ended up "owning the area, especially in regard to image and inventory. When they believed in something, they packed it in." When Lit Brothers closed all stores in April 1977, it created a vacancy at the popular Neshaminy Mall. Carratilo continues:

> *We thought that everything would change when we opened at Neshaminy* [located about ten miles away from the Levittown Shop-a-Rama]. *We thought that everything Lits did wrong, we would do right and explode our business. But we did just as poorly as Lits. When Lits opened, they won all types of architectural and retailing awards for its "ideal layout." But it was not! Usually in department stores, you walked right into cosmetics and jewelry. At the old Lits, ready-to-wear wrapped around the entire first floor, and there were walls dividing up the floor. We didn't do too much in that store, and we had no impulse customers.*

By the late 1970s, Pomeroy's fiercest competitor was Boscov's, which vied for Pomeroy's traditional and moderate core customer base. Al Boscov was

THANK YOU...

We appreciate your purchase and we hope you will be satisfied in every way.

It is our aim to give every Pomeroy customer the best of service, outstanding quality, and real value, and we hope you will be satisfied with your purchase.

In order to make your shopping at Pomeroy's easier and speedier....

Use your **POMEROY'S CHARGE PLATE** whenever you shop...

It saves time.... it protects you... it identifies you.

For over 100 years....thousands of shoppers have learned that it pays to

SHOP

POMEROY'S

A UNIT OF ALLIED STORES CORPORATION   **FIRST**

...whoever you are...whatever you need...whenever you need it

● WILKES-BARRE ● MIDWAY ● WYOMING VALLEY ● POTTSVILLE ● NESHAMINY ●
● LEVITTOWN ● WILLINGBORO ● WILMINGTON ● HARRISBURG ● CAMP HILL ●
● LEBANON ● COLONIAL PARK ● READING ● BERKSHIRE MALL ●

According to the locations listed on its reverse side, this Pomeroy's sales receipt dates from 1979. The slogan "Shop Pomeroy's First" is placed side by side with the statement, "Whoever you are...whatever you need...whenever you need it." *Collection of Lois Witmer.*

known as a "very tough competitor." Ross Ricketts recalls one meeting he had with Boscov. "I remember taking a commuter plane flight from Reading to New York for a meeting, but the flight became delayed. The airline held the plane because Al needed to correct the newspaper ads before they went to the paper!" Boscov's built up its business by broadening its inventory and frequently offering special deals and promotions at its stores. Some people compare Al Boscov's sense of flair and showmanship to Max Hess Jr. in Allentown, Pennsylvania. "Max was wonderful; I adored him," says Boscov. Continuing into 2014, Al Boscov still handles his own advertising. One of his famous and catchy slogans was, "Did You Boscov Today?" Alfred Eisenpreis worked at Allied Stores' corporate office in New York. His wife, Bettijane Long Eisenpreis, recalls that Gertz of Jamaica, Queens, was a division of Allied. "When Boscov's pushed its 'Did You Boscov Today?' promotion, Alfred used to say, 'Have You Gertzed Today?' It just sounded horrible," says Eisenpreis.

To maintain its share of the retail market, Pomeroy's decided to upgrade its image. In 1980, Allied Stores redefined its corporate mission and target customer. "The growing ranks of working women are becoming more aware of fashion—from the Chanel-look suit she may wear to business, to the velour warm-up suit she wears to jog in, to the newest food processor or video disc she may want for her home. [Allied is] upgrading the look, the taste, the quality of everything we sell—clothes, accessories, home furnishings—and at every price level."[109]

Mike Carratilo worked hard to incorporate Estee Lauder cosmetics into Pomeroy's stores. Allied only carried Estee Lauder in its larger stores, such as Jordan Marsh in Boston and Bon Marché in Seattle. "When Estee Lauder became popular, Allied came crawling back on its hands and knees, and Estee Lauder didn't want to listen to Allied," says Carratilo. When a local drugstore in Pottsville closed its doors, it created an opening for a cosmetics distributor in the small city. "The Pottsville Pomeroy's catered to a mixed-income, lower to moderate and older customers, but it became the first Pomeroy's to carry Estee Lauder." When Carratilo was contacted by the cosmetics firm about the new Pottsville opportunity, he thought, "But that's my worst store!" Estee Lauder was loyal to its long-term distributors and was hesitant to expand the brand to its competition. Lauder started in the Pottsville store and was introduced shortly afterward to the Midway store near Wilkes-Barre ("My two worst stores!") before it made its way to downtown Wilkes-Barre and, finally, to the Wyoming Valley Mall store. When he first arrived to manage the Camp Hill store, Ross Ricketts clearly remembers, "Pomeroy's [in Harrisburg] still didn't carry Estee Lauder!"

On November 13, 1980, Strawberry Square celebrated its official grand opening in downtown Harrisburg.[110] A model of urban renewal and redevelopment, Strawberry Square brought first-class office space, a food court and enclosed retail shops to Harrisburg's aging downtown. Pomeroy's building, though not under the ownership or management of the Harristown Development Corporation, was connected to the mixed-use complex. Harristown, the management firm of Strawberry Square, had negotiated to include Bowman's department store into its complex, but the store closed in April 1976. Strawberry Square brought initial excitement to downtown, but "as far as Pomeroy's goes, Strawberry Square didn't amount to much," says Lee Spitalny. And when he was elected Harrisburg's (longtime) mayor in 1982, Stephen Reed knew that reversing downtown Harrisburg's decline was a tall order. "At noon, you could pull up your car and turn off your engine, and just listen. And guess what, you wouldn't hear anything," said Reed in a rare 2014 interview in *Local Quarterly*. "There's no traffic. There are no people. The buildings are all vacant. And nothing."[111] Pomeroy's and the neighboring Strawberry Square project tried to keep downtown Harrisburg alive and relevant during the 1980s, aside from the city's important role as the state capital.

In a 1981 corporate report, Allied Stores stated its mission: "[M]eeting needs of customers, requiring a commitment to pursue a fashion direction that is dictated by our customers and a dedication to provide the best possible service in our stores."[112] The report also recommended the elimination of "stores which are unprofitable or producing an unsatisfactory return." By 1983, only four of Pomeroy's fourteen department stores were located in enclosed shopping malls. Five of its stores were in older downtown buildings, and the remaining branches were housed in suburban open-air shopping plazas.

In an effort to modernize the company, Allied Stores reassessed many of Pomeroy's downtown operations. In the summer of 1983, Pomeroy's closed its "outdated" Pottsville downtown location and opened a new branch at the Schuylkill Mall in Frackville, fifteen minutes north of the city. The Schuylkill Mall had opened in 1980 and slowly siphoned business out of downtown Pottsville. Former Pottsville employee Delores McKenna says, "Once the [Schuylkill] Mall opened up, everybody under fifty went there to shop. You couldn't get kids to go downtown. It destroyed it." Pomeroy's closure in downtown Pottsville came on the heels of the closures of the Sears, Roebuck store and the Necho Allen Hotel.

In 1984, the forty-seven-thousand-square-foot "unprofitable" downtown Lebanon, Pennsylvania location closed its doors. "The Lebanon store was very small," remembers former buyer Pat Eichorn. "It almost felt like a five-and-dime. But Lebanon was a small town. We would bring in merchandise, and it just wouldn't sell, so we'd have to pull it out after a while. The store just didn't do well."

In addition to closing the Pottsville and Lebanon units, Allied Stores Corporation announced, in October 1984, the closure of its A.E. Troutman Company division. Based in the small western Pennsylvania city of Greensburg, Troutman's consisted of a large downtown Greensburg store and seven branches in small communities, most of which had less than fifty thousand square feet. Troutman's was founded in 1897, and its six-story downtown store was largely constructed in 1921. Its closing announcement was a shock to area residents and community leaders. Troutman's closure was cited as "another losing struggle by an American institution—'Main Street'—to earn profits and retain customers against the tremendous people-pulling power of suburban shopping malls."[113]

Two Troutman's stores—at the Westmoreland Mall in Greensburg and the Franklin Mall in Washington, Pennsylvania—were converted to Pomeroy's stores in February 1985. Company officials stated that sales at the downtown Greensburg store had "dropped by nearly two-thirds since the chain opened its biggest store at Westmoreland Mall." Former Reading manager Ross Ricketts states, "Troutman's was an old-time store. It wasn't a high-fashion store, but it had a good basement operation. The store was strong for its area. But downtown Greensburg wasn't much after Troutman's left, that's for sure." Over the years, Pomeroy's and Troutman's worked closely together as members of Allied Stores' Group H merchandising division. News reports called Pomeroy's "a department store that emphasizes name-brand clothing and items for the home. Very similar to Troutman's, Pomeroy's is a bigger concern [and] can bring in some higher-quality merchandise, with more designer items."[114]

On October 5, 1984, Allied Stores announced the closure of the downtown Reading Pomeroy's. The announcement "sent shock waves throughout a city already scarred by massive downtown demolition [from the failed Penn Mall project] and many store closings." In its later years, the store had struggled to remain viable and relevant. "We had closed a few floors off and still maintained it fairly well," says former manager Ross Ricketts, but to no avail. City officials reassured Readingites that Pomeroy's closing was "not a death knell to downtown by any sense of the word."[115] However, by 1984, many shoppers had abandoned downtown Reading as a retailing center. Reading historian George M. Meiser IX recalls Pomeroy's final Christmas in 1984: "I remember standing at the corner of 6th and Penn with my wife, and we were the only two people around. I couldn't believe it. For their last Christmas, [Pomeroy's] just placed these little boxes in their great big windows. I thought, 'Haven't we come down.'"

The downtown Reading store began its "Going Out of Business Sale" on February 15, 1985, and locked its doors on March 2, 1985. The following day, the *Reading Eagle* reported on the store's final day: "All that remains is the macabre remnants of a once-thriving store…and the empty innards of a downtown landmark that, in its early days, was the pinnacle of the city. A

In October 1984, Allied Stores announced the closure of its Troutman's division in western Pennsylvania. The main store in downtown Greensburg was shuttered, and several smaller Troutman's assumed new owners. Two larger Troutman's stores were converted to Pomeroy's. This photograph shows the mall entrance to the Troutman's at Washington, Pennsylvania's Franklin Mall. *Courtesy of the Bon-Ton Stores Inc.*

number of employees milled about in the lobby shaking their heads at the latecomers who missed out on the final-day sale. It was as if [the employees] were delaying the inevitable—the final exit."[116] The closing fit Allied's strategy of "replacing large outdated units" with smaller, efficient suburban stores.[117] Just two months after Reading closed, Pomeroy's opened a modest-sized sixty-thousand-square-foot branch at the Coventry Mall, just south of Pottstown. Many of the 125 Reading employees were offered jobs there, but only a few accepted. Most employees relied on public transportation, and the Coventry Mall store was a twenty-five-minute car trip from downtown Reading.

In June 1986, Allied Stores Corporation purchased ten Gimbels stores from British American Tobacco (BATUS). BATUS had put the entire Gimbels chain up for sale due to declining sales and increased competition. Gimbels catered to moderate-income shoppers, and most of its traditional customer base left for upper-end department stores and boutiques or any of the numerous discount retailers. Allied converted seven of the former Gimbels Philadelphia-area stores to Stern's and its lone Gimbels Lancaster store to Pomeroy's. Located at the popular Park City Mall, Gimbels' Lancaster store opened in September 1971 but failed to develop a loyal audience, especially as it struggled to compete with the locally popular Watt & Shand department store. "Gimbels had a bad reputation in Lancaster," says Ross Ricketts. Pomeroy's was able to build market share in Lancaster because "we modeled the merchandise after our popular Camp Hill store." However, the purchase of the Gimbels and Pomeroy stores was Allied's last independent business decision before it fell victim to the merger mania of the mid-1980s.

Chapter 11

BON VOYAGE

The mid-1980s was a very difficult period for most department store retailers. These businesses were faced with increased competition; large, antiquated buildings; and investors that were more interested in real estate holdings than merchandising. In January 1986, a *Philadelphia Inquirer* news article noted, "Department stores are getting shot at from all sides by specialty stores, off-price chains, discounters, and catalogue merchants. Wounded badly, the big stores are losing shoppers faster than they would like to admit."[118] Successful firms such as the May Department Stores Company and Dillard Department Stores acquired smaller, less profitable retailers in order to increase store count and presence and enjoy volume pricing. Independent department stores largely disappeared, and real estate firms swooped in and purchased valuable land and leases. Robert Campeau was a French Canadian real estate developer who set his sights on the Allied Stores Corporation, Pomeroy's parent company. Allied was a perfect takeover candidate, as the company was blamed for paying "little attention" to its stores and for low-growth and underperforming stores. On September 4, 1986, Campeau made an unsolicited offer of $2.47 billion for Allied Stores.

Campeau's offer was quickly rejected. More determined than ever, he spent the next month planning a hostile takeover of Allied. Campeau was known as a feisty yet soft-spoken man who craved respect. The purchase of Allied Stores would give him the business clout and "social legitimacy" that he sought. His offers increased, and many analysts felt that the bids were excessive and unrealistic. By early October, Allied's board of directors had approved a $3.3 billion purchase of the corporation. By heavily leveraging the deal, Campeau incurred hefty debt payments. To finance the purchase, Campeau sold sixteen of Allied's weaker divisions, including Pomeroy's. Despite his assertion that "[t]he department store has always been here and I think will be here forever," Robert Campeau began to dismantle Allied.

Campeau sold the Levittown and Willingboro stores to Boscov's and began a liquidation sale on December 26, 1986. A few weeks later, the popular Wilmington, Delaware location also became part of Boscov's purchase. The sale of the Levittown store did not surprise local shoppers and industry analysts, but it created fear throughout Pomeroy's Harrisburg executive offices. "The hapless Pomeroy's is but one of the incidental victims of the frenzy of mergers, acquisitions and restructurings sweeping the retail industry…Many Philadelphians haven't heard of Pomeroy's [and] even some Bucks County residents [especially] those young enough to qualify as the 'mall generation' don't know the store," reported the *Philadelphia Inquirer*.[119] Boscov's introduced its Ports-of-the-World concept stores to the Levittown and Willingboro locations. Ports combined the services of a department store with selected off-price merchandise. "It was our way to sneak into the Philadelphia-area market," says Chairman Albert Boscov. Within a few years, the locations had been converted into full-line Boscov's stores, and the company had successfully expanded into Philadelphia.

On February 25, 1987, Campeau announced the closure of the downtown Wilkes-Barre Pomeroy's. A Public Square landmark, the store served older customers, who were alarmed by the announcement. One nineteen-year employee stated, "We had no warning at all that the store was closing. Older customers who don't like shopping at the mall were coming in all day, some were crying, as they asked if it was true that the store was closing."[120] Former personnel director June Bonning says, "The closure was a shock to downtown. The people who shopped at Pomeroy's shopped there forever. Most customers depended on the bus. Many [employees] took retirement. The customers were dedicated to that store, and the store was dedicated to its customers." Headquarters staff in Harrisburg blamed Robert Campeau for compromising Pomeroy's future. "Campeau ruined people's lives," says former credit employee Lois Witmer. "When they announced the sale to Campeau, I kept thinking of the hundreds of people who [would lose their jobs] and have nowhere to go. I also blame the two guys from Allied who probably just casually sat down in a [restaurant] booth and sold the corporation."

After an eight-month period of uncertainty under Robert Campeau's ownership, Pomeroy's announced its purchase by S. Grumbacher & Son,

the longest —— the strongest!
1876 - 1987

An interesting in-house collage shows the Harrisburg Pomeroy's set amongst other local buildings and institutions. The collage notes, "The Longest—The Strongest." The range of dates (1876–1987) refers to the company founding in Reading and the store's acquisition by the Bon-Ton. *Collection of Lois Witmer.*

operator of the Bon-Ton department store chain based in York, Pennsylvania. The agreement was reached on June 18, 1987, and was hailed as "an important strategic step for our company, which will significantly enhance our presence in Pennsylvania," stated Bon-Ton president Tim Grumbacher. The press release continued, "The Pomeroy's stores and the Pomeroy's organization are of recognized high quality and we are enthusiastic about their prospects for future growth. They will continue to offer the same level of quality merchandise and customer service that they have for over 100 years."[121] Retail analyst Kurt Bernard cited the challenges that Bon Ton faced with its new purchase. "Pomeroy's is an old established company that has to get itself a little up to snuff. Mergers have become for many companies a necessity…to cut costs to remain competitive in a market that is increasingly saturated with retail stores."[122] Bernard commented that, as of June 1987, Pomeroy's sales performance per square foot was "way, way below par," at about half the national average for department stores.

Bon-Ton's purchase of Pomeroy's strained relations within the family-run business. "It became clear that [the Bon-Ton] had to grow, or we weren't going to survive," says Bon-Ton CEO Tim Grumbacher. "My father [Tom Grumbacher] was frugal until the day he died. He never wanted to borrow any money." The Grumbacher family had agreed to submit to binding arbitration if there were any business disagreements.[123] When the company borrowed about $90 million to purchase Pomeroy's from the Campeau Corporation, "My father couldn't be a part of it, so he stepped down from the active management of the business. He only wanted to buy the good [Pomeroy's] stores, not the headaches." The company's acquisition of Pomeroy's was the first of many for the Bon-Ton organization. Over the next several years, Bon-Ton acquired Adam, Meldrum & Anderson (Buffalo), McCurdy's (Rochester), Chappell's (Syracuse) and twenty Hess's stores based in Allentown, Pennsylvania. Although he opposed the initial Pomeroy's purchase, Tom Grumbacher kept a note in his desk drawer that stated, "There is no security in this world, just opportunity." His son, Tim, capitalized on that opportunity and built the Bon-Ton Department Stores Inc. into a retailing powerhouse.

Soon after the Bon-Ton purchase, the Lancaster, Pennsylvania Pomeroy's was sold to Boscov's. The decision was based on a gentlemen's agreement between Lancaster's Watt & Shand department store and the Bon-Ton stores to never compete against each other. "We [Bon-Ton] sold it to Boscov's because we knew that we were eventually going to get Watt & Shand," says former manager Ross Ricketts. And in February 1992, Bon-Ton did formally acquire Lancaster's two Watt & Shand stores. As the Bon-Ton grew, the company experienced its share of growing pains. Bon-Ton's stores typically ran 60,000 to 80,000 square feet in size, while stores of Pomeroy's and Watt & Shand were as large as 150,000 square feet.[124] It took several years before Bon-Ton comfortably brought larger-sized stores into its corporate footprint. The firm realized that larger stores "must be more things to more people."[125]

Although Bon-Ton claimed to be committed to the Pomeroy's name and Bon-Ton president Tim Grumbacher stressed that his company would operate each division separately, Bon-Ton slowly merged Pomeroy's

After the Bon-Ton Stores acquired Pomeroy's, the company documented the interior of the downtown Harrisburg store. This photograph of the first-floor men's store shows the mezzanine tearoom and its covered windows. *Courtesy of the Bon-Ton Stores Inc.*

Fake trees decorated the downtown Harrisburg Pomeroy's children's department in 1987. *Courtesy of the Bon-Ton Stores Inc.*

Left: An antiquated piping and wiring system adorns the ceiling of the housewares department in Harrisburg. Allied Stores' private-label Belgique cookware is advertised as part of Pomeroy Days in 1987. *Courtesy of the Bon-Ton Stores Inc.*

Below: The windows of Harrisburg's mezzanine Tea Room can be seen in the background of this photograph. *Courtesy of the Bon-Ton Stores Inc.*

This collection of the various Pomeroy's credit cards shows the many different designs over the years. The card on the bottom right depicts the font used after the acquisition by the Bon-Ton Stores. *Collection of Lois Witmer.*

Harrisburg executive offices with Bon-Ton's headquarters staff in York over the next two years. By March 1989, all Pomeroy's advertising, sales promotion and merchandising staffs were handled out of York, and the merger was complete. Although the stores still operated under their separate nameplates, Bon-Ton leadership announced, "We are treating the company as one now. Everything will be run out of the York store."[126]

Lee Spitalny's husband, Howard, was the Harrisburg store manager under Bon-Ton's leadership and frequently traveled to York. "Howard always said that he loved retailing with a passion until computers came along," says Spitalny. "When Pomeroy's transferred to Bon-Ton, computers were everywhere. He felt, 'What are the computer's feelings? They're all about numbers'!" Regardless, Howard Spitalny enjoyed most of his time with Bon-Ton and "had a lot of friends in York." Lee Spitalny continues, "Howard was very attached to Pomeroy's, but he was not as nostalgic as some people. He knew that it was a job to do." Thirty-two-year veteran credit department employee Lois Witmer worked at the downtown Harrisburg Pomeroy's until Bon-Ton moved the staff to York. Like a number of her colleagues, Witmer left the company because she didn't have transportation to get to York.

On October 16, 1989, Bon-Ton announced the closure of the Strawberry Square downtown Harrisburg Pomeroy's due to declining sales. The store was the last vestige of the venerable Pomeroy company, and many longtime Harrisburgers mourned the decision. City officials denounced the store's

A Pomeroy's sale brochure from November 1987 shows a model in front of the Harrisburg Central Railroad Station. *Collection of Lois Witmer.*

impending demise. Mayor Stephen Reed said, "[Bon-Ton] caused the store's poor sales by failing to stock it with good merchandise and market it to the public."[127] Russ Ford, senior vice-president of Harristown Development Corporation, Strawberry Square's developer, stated, "Strawberry Square [became] more important to Pomeroy's than Pomeroy's was to Strawberry Square."[128] The management of the complex called Pomeroy's departure "a poor business decision" but added that the store didn't do too much to

On August 27, 1989, the two department store companies formally merged and were officially renamed "The Bon-Ton/Pomeroy's." On August 12, 1990, all stores assumed the Bon-Ton nameplate. *Collection of the author.*

"stimulate downtown shopping." The management further noted that more visitors entered Strawberry Square from its outside doors than through Pomeroy's direct entrance. One Pomeroy employee felt Bon-Ton's ownership "let her hometown down."

But to some employees, the store's closing seemed inevitable. Bon-Ton CEO Tim Grumbacher understood the outcry toward the store's closure. "Pomeroy's was *the* department store of Harrisburg. Anybody can tell you that there is disappointment when a store closes. People are very attached to these names," he says. He also comments that many department store companies were "not run aggressively" and "had their feet stuck in concrete."[129] Many companies were hesitant to give up on their downtown stores. "Toward the end under Bon-Ton, the downtown Pomeroy's had shrunk, and entire floors were closed," states buyer Carol Brightbill. "It just wasn't what the store used to be." Without any fanfare, the downtown store closed on January 6, 1990. All unsold merchandise was sent to other Bon-Ton locations. The closure was especially hard on senior citizens and Harrisburgers who had been loyal to the local store throughout the years. Former employee Mary Custer says, "I was really upset about Pomeroy's closing. It was terrible not to be able to shop downtown." Another employee, Ann Johnson, quipped on the store's final day, "I've been shopping at least forty-eight years here, and any time anyone would ask me where I bought something, I would always say 'Pomeroy's—where else?'"[130]

After sitting dormant for two years, demolition began on the downtown Harrisburg store. The process was expected to take one week. However, the demolition firm soon discovered that the structure was stronger and more solid than initially expected. The *Patriot-News* commented, "Although the cornerstone of downtown Harrisburg shopping has put up a heck of a fight, forcing two extensions in the estimated demolition timetable, the wrecking ball eventually will win out. It's kind of like the U.S. Olympic basketball team vs. Argentina. There was never really any doubt who would win."[131] The demolition continued into the fall, and many pieces of the building were saved and recycled for future construction projects. Lois Witmer, a longtime worker in the store's credit department, felt "terrible" when the downtown Pomeroy's closed. "But I felt even worse when it was torn down! That was the worst because you knew that it was going to be gone forever." Witmer expands on this sentiment in a personal essay titled "The Last Words of a Landmark":

> *On May 30, 1992, they began to tear me down. The television cameras were rolling from all the local stations and the newspaper reporters were here to watch and report as they tried to demolish me. I will not surrender easily for my structure was made to last for generations. Emptiness and destruction can only occur when caring ceases in the hearts and minds of thoughtless human beings. All the money for demolition and then to rebuild wasn't enough to reconstruct or renovate my appearance. Therefore, I cannot be saved from the cement pendulum beating away in slow motion at my foundation or the large*

The view of Pomeroy's along Market Street in Harrisburg became quiet and dated by the late 1980s. *Collection of Lois Witmer.*

One of the earliest sections that made up the downtown Harrisburg Pomeroy's received an updated storefront in the mid-1950s. *Collection of Lois Witmer.*

Demolition of the downtown Harrisburg Pomeroy's officially began in May 1992. The site was initially cleared for use as a parking lot. *Collection of Lois Witmer.*

After sitting dormant in the center of the city for more than a decade, the downtown Reading Pomeroy's was finally demolished in April 1995. *Collection of Leonard Miller.*

claw mouth that chews into my interior. In a few short weeks I'll be gone, but I hope not forgotten. While I was here a lot of good times were had and shared. Thanks to the people who do care, I'm positive those memories created will live on for many, many years to come.

The situation was not much different at the former downtown Reading store. Although the former Harrisburg store was destined to become a parking lot, numerous attempts were made to repurpose the Reading location after its closure in 1985. The building's ownership passed back and forth between developers and investors. Plans called for converting the former department store into a shopping complex, an apartment building or an office complex, but none was seen as "viable" and cost effective.[132] Any redevelopment efforts were hampered by the building's immediate surroundings. It sat alongside blocks of businesses that had been leveled in 1974, creating an eyesore in the heart of Reading's downtown. "It was a disaster once they tore down in the 500–700 blocks of Penn Street [back in 1974]," says Boscov's chairman Albert Boscov. "They were very big blocks that were home to many smaller specialty stores. It created in hole in the city and downtown was no longer a major draw."

Although it acquired historic status and public campaigns crusaded to block its demise, demolition on the Pomeroy building began in April 1995. Pomeroy family member Barbara Korczykowski did not watch the former store get torn down. "I saw some of the news articles, but I just couldn't read all of them." Another family member, James Seivers, recalls that the Pomeroy family was not happy about the company's sale to Bon-Ton for "sentimental reasons." Seivers adds, "The downtown store was a very handsome building. [Now that it's gone] there should at least be a plaque." Within two years, the corner of Sixth and Penn Streets had become home to a regional bank headquarters.

Along with the former Reading and Harrisburg locations, other shuttered downtown Pomeroy's were eventually repurposed. The Pottsville Pomeroy's closed in 1983 and opened two years later as a Treadway Inn, now branded as a Ramada Hotel. The "Mighty Pomeroy's" conversion to a hotel helped fill a void in downtown lodging since the Necho Allen Hotel closed in 1981.[133] The former downtown Easton store sat dormant for years after its closure in 1976. With the site reborn in 2012 as a multipurpose facility, the *Easton Express-Times* reported, "After 35 years of good ideas and failed plans, Easton's biggest and most achingly vacant retail property opened its doors to commercial and residential tenants. Part of the city's soul was quarantined when department stores and other businesses fled in the 1970s. The reclamation of Pomeroy's isn't the foundation on which all of the downtown's revitalization depends—it's important, but it's one of many. That's a good sign for a downtown that struggled for so long."[134]

The redevelopment of the historic former Wilkes-Barre Pomeroy's, prominently located on Public Square, was the subject of long-term debate. After it closed on June 1987, the building stood "dormant for nearly six years, the floors buckled, sections of the ceiling caved in, and gaping holes in the roof allowed torrents of storm water to flow freely into through the building."[135] Its condition evoked nostalgia and concern by local residents. Historian Tom Mooney remembers shopping in the Wilkes-Barre store, which was his late mother's favorite:

> *While it shared many characteristics with other stores (such as the system of tubes for cashiers), it was taller (five stories plus a basement) than the others, and it had that strange bent shape. I never saw an escalator in there—just stairs and elevators. The steps were in a stairwell on one side of the building. Its show windows used a minimalist style, unlike the lavish styles of other stores. It was also a complete department store, unlike its Bon-Ton successor, which is fixated on clothing.*

The building, whose ownership left Pomeroy company hands in 1955, was foreclosed on in 1990 and was purchased at auction on December 27, 1991. The Greater Wilkes-Barre Partnership acquired the building, and its rebirth was spearheaded by an $8.5 million redevelopment venture supported by public and private funding. The restoration included the removal of the façade panels but did not include the replacement of its former triangularly shaped rooftop. The former Pomeroy's, rebranded as Public Square Commons, was reopened on March 9, 1995, as an office, educational and commercial complex that retained many of the department store's distinctive features. The *Citizens' Voice* newspaper reported, "Those who remember walking from department to department of Pomeroy's probably remember

Opposite, top: In 1992, the shuttered downtown Wilkes-Barre location began a lengthy restoration. After its 1960s-era panels were removed, the original Jonas Long's Sons nameplate was discovered. *Courtesy of the Greater Wilkes-Barre Chamber of Commerce.*

Opposite, bottom: After a painstaking restoration, the former downtown Wilkes-Barre store was reopened in March 1995 as "Public Square Commons." *Photograph by the author.*

Downtown Wilkes-Barre's Boston Store continues to operate under the Boscov's name. It is one of the few downtown department stores currently operating in the country. *Photograph by the author.*

the sea-legs needed to traverse its wavy floors. Despite the building's multi-million dollar restoration, the floor is still as uneven as ever. While many taxpayers may be disheartened to know the hefty bill did nothing to level the floor, those who nostalgically remember shopping the old city landmark may find retention of the structural quirk almost charming." Regardless of its new name and purpose, Public Square Commons is referred to by many of the local residents as "the Old Pomeroy's." "It'll always be Pomeroy's," says Chamber of Commerce employee John Maday.

Wilkes-Barre has the distinction of being home to a rare downtown department store. The former Fowler, Dick & Walker—The Boston Store operates as a full-service Boscov's on South Main Street. Boscov's remains committed to the downtown, and Chairman Al Boscov feels that downtown Wilkes-Barre is coming back. "We think that we can build the business again. Wilkes-Barre hopefully has a good future, and it is still making money," he said. Tom Mooney describes the Boscov's/Boston Store downtown operation:

[The downtown Boscov's] *is somewhat of an anomaly—a traditional-looking, four-story department store with a basement, giving it five floors of sales space. One reason for its endurance is likely its adaptability. Early in the twentieth century, it began expanding into nearby buildings and developing special-interest areas, such as its Grey Shoppes for fashion merchandise and a mockup of a small home to display various home furnishings in a real-life setting. It also had a large bargain basement. The store was an early proponent of elevators, escalators (which in themselves drew spectators), a full-service dining room and its own parkade.*

Albert Boscov also remains committed to downtown Reading. "We are trying to bring Reading back with apartments and hotels. But I don't know if it will work for a department store."

In 1968, Pomeroy's published an in-house booklet titled *Pomeroy's: An Enchanting Story with the Pennsylvania Touch*. In addition to various facts and figures, it discussed the company's mission, merchandise and geographical location:

Tradition stands, beauty abounds, wherever you tour. Covered bridges, hallowed battle grounds, ancient but well-tended barns and farm houses dot the landscape surrounded by colorful, tree-shaded rolling hills covering over 50% of the state. That's the beauty of Pomeroy's territory.

Of greater importance is the dynamic upward trend of its people towards the full life that permeates Pomeroy's market area. Behind the Sylvania atmosphere dollar and cents figures dramatically emphasize the productivity and prosperity of Pomeroy's families. And most important, Pomeroy's has located attractive, modern department stores right in the centers of 2.2 million affluent families—totaling over 7.5 million people who have long learned it pays to look to Pomeroy's for everything they need for gracious living. Pomeroy's views the future of its territory with enthusiastic optimism and is dedicated to the area's growth and its customer's needs.

Whether customers are looking for the latest in high fashions, unusual gifts, household furnishings, sportswear, men's wear or clothes for the children, they know they can find just what they want, in a wide assortment at the right price at Pomeroy's.

In the early 1980s, Allied Stores Corporation, Pomeroy's parent company, approached Bon-Ton (in York) and wanted to buy its stores. The Grumbacher family declined. "We were having too much fun. The department store business was exciting and constantly changing," states

Above: The former Camp Hill Pomeroy's still operates as a successful branch of the Bon-Ton Stores. *Photograph by the author.*

Left: In 1968, Pomeroy's Inc. produced a brief corporate historical and analytical report titled *Pomeroy's: An Enchanting Story with the Pennsylvania Touch*. *Collection of Lois Witmer.*

Tim Grumbacher. In 2005, Bon-Ton purchased the stores that belonged to Chicago's Carson, Pirie, Scott & Company group. Carson's corporate office operated such names as the Boston Store (Milwaukee), Bergner's (Peoria) and Younkers (Des Moines), along with its own iconic Chicago stores. However, by that time, Tim's father, Tom Grumbacher, was suffering from Alzheimer's disease. "I remember telling my father to look at these names [that the Bon-Ton now controlled]! I hope that he knew it."

When Grumbacher reflects on the 1987 acquisition of Pomeroy's, he understands that his company did not just purchase another department store; he "acquired a tradition":

> *Department stores were where people loved to meet, eat in the tearooms, talk to sales associates, seek advice and hear gossip. It's still the case in our stores. That's the key.* [The Bon-Ton] *feels that there is there is still a need for people to have social outings. We are doing our best, and we believe that this is still important to our customers.*

Tim Grumbacher feels that his company has worked hard at keeping the Pomeroy's tradition alive. "Many former Pomeroy's employees are still with us," he said. And he also gives industry credit to Al Boscov, a "retailing legend who is good at everything with running a retail store."

In the 1930s, Pomeroy's was the dominant department store business in central and eastern Pennsylvania. Every Pomeroy city, from Pottsville to Wilkes-Barre to Harrisburg, had its own story to tell. But the company traced its origins to Reading. When the doors of the downtown Reading store closed on March 3, 1985, the *Reading Eagle* commented, "Pomeroy's is Real Reading. Always has been. Through the years, Pomeroy's, without fanfare, was the hub of shopping in Reading. While it was less flamboyant in its advertising policies than the modern Boscov's, and less exclusive than Whitner's in its merchandise, Pomeroy's certainly delivered the goods."[136] Generations of residents and loyal customers always knew to "Shop Pomeroy's First."

SHOPPER'S SPECIAL

In 1958, Pomeroy's Reading Tea Room head chef Theodore Poulios commented on his restaurant's patrons in the *Reading Eagle* newspaper: "Berks County women never deviate in one respect—they want quality food at reasonable prices." He said that the Tea Room "caters almost exclusively to the woman shopper who does not insist of the superfluous frills which go into food preparation in similar establishments elsewhere. They like their food to be attractive but they willingly forgo a few extra touches in favor of a more reasonable price."[137]

DEVILED EGGS

3 hard-cooked eggs
1 tablespoon sour cream or mayonnaise
2 tablespoons deviled ham

Cut hard-cooked eggs in half crosswise and remove the yolk. Blend the yolks with sour cream or mayonnaise and deviled ham. Refill.

CHEESE POTATOES

3 tablespoons melted butter
4 medium-size potatoes
⅔ cup corn flakes
½ cup finely grated cheese
½ teaspoon paprika
I teaspoon salt

Pour 2 tablespoons of butter into a shallow baking dish. Cut potatoes into ½-inch slices and place close together in pan. Brush tops of potatoes with remaining butter. Roll corn flakes into fine crumbs and combine with cheese, paprika and salt. Sprinkle over the potatoes. Bake for 15 minutes in a moderate oven. Serves 4.

PEPPER ONION RELISH

6 onions, chopped fine
12 green peppers, chopped fine
½ cup parsley
I cup sugar
2 teaspoons salt
2 cups wine vinegar

Place the onions, peppers and parsley into boiling water. Cover, allow the ingredients to stand for 5 minutes and then drain. After vegetables are drained, add sugar, salt and vinegar. Boil for ½ hour and put up in jar.

Fresh Country Egg Omelette

2 eggs
2 tablespoons milk
salt, to taste

2 tablespoons butter
1–2 slices yellow American cheese
grape jelly

Whisk eggs, milk and salt in metal mixing bowl. In an 8-inch skillet, heat butter until melted. Add eggs/milk until mixture begins to set. Do not flip. Omelette is to be served open faced. Place cheese slices in center of eggs. Place the omelette under a broiler for no longer than one minute, or until cheese begins to bubble. Once set, spread grape jelly on top of omelette.

Scotch Woodcock

A popular cheddar cheese dish, Scotch Woodcock was featured on the menu in 1958 and "proved a favorite with women shoppers who patronized the local establishment."

3 tablespoons flour
2 tablespoons butter
1 quart hot milk
¼ pound Canadian cheddar
   cheese
¼ pound white American cheese
1 teaspoon salt
2 teaspoons dry mustard

2 teaspoons Worcestershire sauce
1 cup pimentos, chopped
1 cup green peppers, chopped
2 cups mushrooms, chopped
slices of bread, toasted and cut
   into halves
2 strips bacon, cooked

Blend the flour and butter and heat. Add the quart of hot milk and continue heating until the sauce begins to boil. Add the diced cheese, salt, mustard and Worcestershire sauce. Cook until the cheese melts and the mixture has the consistency of heavy cream.

In the meantime, sauté pimentos, peppers and mushrooms in a pan. Add the cheese mixture to the pimento mixture and heat again for about 5 minutes. Ladle over toast halves. Place two strips of bacon over each of the 6 servings.

Pomeroy's operated simple and casual eateries in its department stores, such as the Coffee Pot at the downtown Wilkes-Barre store. *Collection of the Luzerne County Historical Society.*

PINEAPPLE BETTY

½ medium-size fresh pineapple
¼ cup sugar
¾ cup boiling water
2 tablespoons butter
1 cup of stale cake crumbs

Cut the pineapple into ¼-inch slices and peel. Boil sugar and water for 5 minutes. Add the pineapple and cook until tender. Butter a baking pan, cover with cake crumbs and add a layer of pineapple, drained from the juice. Dot the layer with butter and add another layer of crumbs and pineapple. Reserve enough crumbs for the top layer. Pour pineapple juice over the mixture and bake for about 45 minutes in a moderate oven. Serve with hard sauce.

NOTES

CHAPTER 1

1. *Reading Times*, "Pomeroy's Founded by Trio of Salesmen 57 Years Ago," April 26, 1933.
2. *Reading Times*, "George Strickland Pomeroy," obituary, September 14, 1925.
3. *Reading Times*, "How Can Penn Square Be Improved?" June 2, 1871.
4. *Pomeroy's: An Enchanting Story with the Pennsylvania Touch* (Harrisburg, PA: Pomeroy's Inc., 1968).
5. *Harrisburg Telegraph*, "First Big Patron of Pomeroy's Inc., Tells of Steady Growth of Store," September 10, 1928.
6. *Reading Times*, "Dives, Pomeroy & Stewart's New Store," January 21, 1880.
7. Irvin Rathman, "The Gray Lady of Penn Square," *Historical Review of Berks County* (Spring 2001): 59.
8. "Historic Preservation Certification Application," Stahl and Associates, Boston, 1986; Ed Swoyer, Reading Center City Development Fund.
9. *Reading Times*, "A Story of Success," October 3, 1892.
10. *Reading Times*, "46 Years for the Big Store," April 20, 1922.
11. "Historic Preservation Certification Application," 1986.
12. *Reading Times*, "An Auspicious Opening," May 10, 1901.
13. *Reading Times*, "Opening Day Advertisement," May 9, 1901.
14. Rathman, "Gray Lady of Penn Square," 63.

15. *Reading Times*, "Store Tablet Is Unveiled; Exercises Commence Completion of the New Dives, Pomeroy & Stewart Building," December 6, 1922.

Chapter 2

16. *Harrisburg Telegraph*, September 10, 1928.
17. *Harrisburg Telegraph*, "57 Years of Remarkable Progress to Be Celebrated by Pomeroy's," March 21, 1935.
18. *Reading Times*, "Death of Dives, Pomeroy & Stewart Store Manager," September 14, 1922.
19. *Harrisburg Telegraph*, "37th Anniversary Sale," September 20, 1915.
20. *Harrisburg Telegraph*, September 10, 1928.
21. *Harrisburg Telegraph*, "Dives, Pomeroy & Stewart," January 18, 1896.
22. Ibid.
23. *Harrisburg Telegraph*, "Dives, Pomeroy & Stewart's Magnificent Display," December 21, 1893.
24. Lois Witmer, "The Last Words of a Landmark," 1992.
25. *Harrisburg Telegraph*, "Largest Crowds in Store History Attend Industrial Exposition," March 10, 1908.
26. *Reading Eagle*, "Honor of Manager of the Dives, Pomeroy & Stewart Store in Pottstown," May 14, 1914.
27. *Reading Eagle*, "Pomeroy Firm Sells Pottstown Property," December 14, 1928.
28. *History of the County of Schuylkill*, Schuylkill County centenary booklet, 1911.
29. *Altoona Mirror*, "William F. Gable to Observe 70th Anniversary," February 24, 1954.
30. David Sullivan, correspondence with the author, May 16, 1914.
31. *Altoona Mirror*, "Remarkable Life of Store Founder," September 3, 1929.

Chapter 3

32. *Pomeroy's Booster*, July 1923.

33. *Harrisburg Telegraph*, "George Pomeroy, Head of Stores, Dies at Reading," September 14, 1925.

34. *Reading Eagle*, "Pomeroy Will Leaves Estate to Widow and Three Children," September 18, 1925.

35. Rathman, "Gray Lady of Penn Square," 65.

36. Witmer, "Last Words of a Landmark," 1992.

37. *Celebrating Wilkes-Barre's Bicentennial: 1806–2006* (Luzerne, PA: Luzerne Foundation, 2006).

38. *Wilkes-Barre Evening News*, "Pomeroy's Better Dress Department," September 10, 1955.

Chapter 4

39. Pennsylvania Historical and Museum Commission, "Pennsylvania and the Great Depression," 2011.

40. *Reading Eagle*, "Penn Street Store Changes Managers," March 30, 1935.

41. *Pomeroy's: An Enchanting Story*.

42. *Harrisburg Telegraph*, "Greater Pomeroy's Opens Tonight," November 15, 1939.

43. *Reading Eagle*, "Chef at Pomeroy's Tea Room Must Please Shoppers," April 27, 1958.

Chapter 5

44. Ralph W. Kinsey, *50 Years of the History of Pomeroy's, Inc.—1876–1926*, company brochure.

45. *Pomeroy Booster*, in-store employee newsletter, April 1923.

46. *Reading Eagle*, "Pomeroy Players Please in Initial Performance," October 21, 1939.

47. *Harrisburg Telegraph*, "Store Chorus Entertained," January 4, 1934.

48. *Reading Eagle*, "Pomeroy Day," company advertisement, March 2, 1933.

49. *Wilkes-Barre Evening News*, "The Greatest One Day Sale of the Spring Season," company advertisement, March 4, 1938.

50. *Wilkes-Barre Evening News*, company advertisement, November 6, 1948.

CHAPTER 6

51. *Brockton Enterprise*, "James Edgar's Santa Claus—The Spirit of Christmas," November 16, 2008.

52. *Reading Eagle*, "Santa Class," October 19, 1950.

53. *Reading Eagle*, "Christmas Spirit Is a Predominating Feature in Penn Street Stores," December 13, 1908.

54. *Reading Eagle*, "Pomeroy's Fabled Toyland," December 10, 2006.

55. Ray Koehler, "Gray Lady of Penn Square Laid to Rest," *Reading Eagle*, March 3, 1985.

56. *Pottstown Mercury*, "Raggedy Belsnickel Was Early Gift Bearer," December 6, 1972.

CHAPTER 7

57. *Harrisburg Telegraph*, "75th Anniversary of Bowman's Store Will Be Celebrated during Month," June 3, 1946.

58. *Harrisburg Patriot-News*, "Bowman's Was More than a Store," February 22, 1999.

59. *Harrisburg Patriot-News*, "Shop Carried 'Piece of Fifth Avenue'—Mary Sachs' Store Provided Anchor to Fashionable Third Street Row," June 21, 1999.

60. *Harrisburg Patriot-News*, "The Merchant Princess—Exhibit Displays Sachs' Style, Taste," March 25, 2007.

61. *Mercantile Stores Company: A Profile of a Growing Retail Enterprise* (Cincinnati, OH: Mercantile Stores, 1975).

62. John Anderson, "The Lazarus Store: It's a Time for Tears," *Wilkes-Barre Times Leader*, December 26, 1979.

63. Ibid.

64. Mark L. Hoffman, "Lazarus Store Staying in Wilkes-Barre," *Wilkes-Barre Times Leader*, September 1, 1979.

65. Mark L. Hoffman, "Announcement Shocks Downtown Merchants," *Wilkes-Barre Times Leader*, December 28, 1979.

66. *Sunday Independent*, "Isaac Long's Turns Its Best Face Forward," May 1963.

67. Loraine Luke, "The Boston Store Marks 100 Years of Expansion," *Citizens' Voice*, July 12, 1979.

68. *Reading Times*, "Misfortune," May 27, 1911.

69. *Pottstown Mercury*, "Ellis Mills Founds Store on Honesty, Integrity," March 26, 1973.

70. *Berksiana*, "A Random Harvest—Conversations with Solomon Boscov," n.d.

71. F. Alan Shirk, "Fire Hits Firm for a Second Time," *Reading Eagle*, November 21, 1967.

CHAPTER 8

72. Allied Stores Corporation Annual Report, 1963.

73. *Reading Eagle*, "Santa Will Open Moving Stairways," December 7, 1950.

74. *Wilkes-Barre Times Leader*, "Pomeroy's Starts Building Program," February 5, 1954.

75. *Wilkes-Barre Times Leader*, "Mayor Lauds Pomeroy's as Credit to City," September 1, 1955.

76. Pennsylvania Historical and Museum Commission, "Levittown Historical Marker," 1992.

77. *Bucks County Times*, "Pomeroy's Director to Conduct Survey," November 30, 1954.

78. Personal conversation with Lee Starr, June 17, 2014.

79. *Bucks County Times*, "Survey Shows Quality Items Are in Demand," November 4, 1955.

CHAPTER 9

80. *Harrisburg Patriot-News*, "Company Test Pilot Party Advertisement," September 25, 1959.

81. *Wilkes-Barre Record*, "Modernized Front for Pomeroy's," October 29, 1959.

82. Ibid.

83. *Reading Eagle*, "Renovation Phase Completed," December 7, 1962.

84. Allied Stores Corporation Annual Report, 1979.

85. *Reading Eagle*, "Pomeroy's Executive Training Program Is Your Answer," March 28, 1965.

86. *Harrisburg Patriot-News*, "Store's Aim: 'Building Executives,'" October 10, 1968.

87. Dan W. Dodson, New York University Center for Human Relations film, Dynamic Films, 1957.

88. *Lebanon Daily News*, "Grand Opening of Pomeroy's Is Set for Thursday," September 11, 1963.

89. Private conversation with Lee Starr, June 17, 2014.

90. *Lebanon Daily News*, "Throngs Jam Pomeroy's for Grand Opening of $1 Million Renovations," September 13, 1963.

91. *Reading Eagle*, "Laubach's to Be Taken Over August 1," July 3, 1964.

92. Jim Deegan, "Laubach's Should Never Be Forgotten," *Easton Express-Times*, February 25, 2007.

93. Kevin Sylvester, Levittown Beyond website, 2012, http://www.levittownbeyond.com.

94. *Philadelphia Inquirer*, "Pomeroy's Store Opens Friday at Willingboro," August 12, 1965.

95. *Wilkes-Barre Record*, "Pomeroy's to Open Branch at Wyoming," July 16, 1965.

96. Allied Stores Corporation Annual Report, 1979.

97. *Reading Eagle*, "Proposals of a Downtown Reading Mall Becoming Commonplace," February 21, 1967.

98. Allied Stores Corporation Annual Report, 1971.

99. *Harrisburg Patriot-News*, "Pomeroy's Will Be Opening in Fastest Growing Area," October 10, 1968.

100. *Reading Eagle*, "Pomeroy's to Modernize Basement," August 9, 1970.

101. Allied Stores Corporation Annual Report, 1969.

102. *Wilmington Evening Journal*, "Concord Mall to Double in Size," April 1, 1971.

103. Personal conversation with Lee Starr, June 17, 2014.

CHAPTER 10

104. Jim Fulbright, *Flood-PA 1972* (Harrisburg, PA: TV Host magazine, 1972).

105. John J. Rygiel and Paul W. Warnagiris, *The Great Flood of 1972* (Wyoming, PA: Observer-Rygiel Publishing, 1973).

106. Ibid.

107. Mary O. Bradley, "Downtown Department Stores Once Were Top Holiday Destinations," *Harrisburg Patriot-News*, November 22, 2005.

108. *Reading Eagle*, "Pomeroy's Will Remain Downtown," December 12, 1975.

109. Allied Stores Corporation Annual Report, 1980.

110. Paul B. Beers, *City Contented, City Discontented: A History of Modern Harrisburg* (University Park: Pennsylvania State University Press, 2011).

111. Daniel Webster Jr., "Harrisburg: The City Steve Reed Built," *Local Quarterly* 4 (2014).

112. Allied Stores Corporation Annual Report, 1981.

113. Jack Markowitz, "Troutman's Set to Close Stores," *Greensburg Tribune Review*, October 2, 1984.

114. *Pittsburgh Press*, "Pomeroy's Store Opening at Troutman's Site," February 3, 1985.

115. "Historic Preservation Certification Application," 1986.

116. Donald J. Botch, "Final Exit—End of an Era," *Reading Eagle*, March 3, 1985.

117. Allied Stores Annual Report, 1984.

CHAPTER 11

118. Jennifer Lin, "Illness Afflicting Gimbels Is a Common One," *Philadelphia Inquirer*, January 19, 1986.

119. Barbara Demick, "Department Stores Facing New Challenges for Survival," *Philadelphia Inquirer*, January 12, 1987.

120. *Citizens' Voice*, "Wilkes-Barre Pomeroy's Store Will Close," February 26, 1987.

121. Mary Warner, "City-Based Unit Being Resold," *Harrisburg Patriot-News*, June 19, 1987.

122. Ibid.

123. Personal conversation with Tim Grumbacher, June 10, 2014.

124. Nancy Elizabeth Cohen, *Doing a Good Business: 100 Years at the Bon-Ton* (Lyme, CT: Greenwich Publishing, 1998), 58.

125. Ibid.

126. Constance Walker, "Merger of Bon-Ton, Pomeroy's Allows Increase in Staff of York Mall Store," *York Daily Record*, March 1, 1989.

127. Mary Warner, "Pomeroy's in Downtown to Shut Doors," *Harrisburg Patriot-News*, October 17, 1989.

128. Mary Warner, "City Ponders Post-Pomeroy's Era," *Harrisburg Patriot-News*, October 22, 1989.

129. Personal conversation with Tim Grumbacher, June 10, 2014.

130. Jack Sherzer, "Shoppers Reminisce as Pomeroy's Closes Doors," *Harrisburg Patriot-News*, January 7, 1990.

131. Mike Feely, "Demolition Watch," *Harrisburg Patriot-News*, July 4, 1992.

132. *Reading Eagle*, "Pomeroy's Site for Sale," August 13, 1991.

133. *Pottsville Republican Herald*, "Time Changes Many Things," November 15, 2009.

134. *Easton Express-Times*, "Reopening of Pomeroy's Building a Benchmark for Downtown Easton," May 22, 2012.

135. Bill Peace, "Pomeroy's Project Going Down to the Wire," *Wilkes-Barre Times Leader*, January 15, 1995.

136. Ray Koehler, "Gray Lady of Penn Square Laid to Rest," *Reading Eagle*, March 3, 1985.

APPENDIX

137. *Reading Eagle*, "Chef at Pomeroy's Tea Room Must Please Shoppers," April 27, 1958.

INDEX

A

Allied Stores Corporation 45, 46, 54,
  73, 82, 85, 86, 90, 91, 96, 99,
  102, 108, 114, 115, 118, 119,
  121, 123, 139

B

Bamberger's 116
Becker, Shirley 24, 46, 50, 53, 58, 62,
  77, 115
Bennethum, William H. 25
Berkshire Mall 78, 79, 107, 109, 114,
  115
Bernard, Kurt 125, 126
Bonning, June 57, 59, 112, 124
Bon Ton (Lebanon store) 87, 99, 101
Bon-Ton Stores (York, Pennsylvania)
  99, 125, 126, 129, 130, 132,
  135, 136, 139, 141
Boscov, Albert 76, 79, 135, 141
Boscov's 75, 76, 79, 116, 124, 126, 138
Boscov, Solomon 78
Boston Store 40, 75, 76, 96, 109, 138,
  141
Bowman & Company 69, 70, 73, 113,
  118

Brightbill, Carol 53, 70, 102, 108, 112,
  116, 132
Brown, Thomson & Company
  (Hartford store) 17, 44
Buchter, Harold 101

C

Campeau, Robert 123, 124, 126
Camp Hill (store) 107, 108, 109, 112,
  113, 118, 122
Carratilo, Mike 45, 54, 74, 76, 90, 109,
  111, 116, 118
Carson, Pirie, Scott & Company 141
cash-ball system
  Harrisburg 28
  Reading 19
Colarusso, Joseph R. 114, 115
Colonial Park (store) 112, 113
Concord Mall (store) 109, 124
Coons, Albert 46, 99, 101, 115
Coventry Mall (store) 121
Custer, Mary 64, 108, 132

D

Debenham & Freebody (London store) 17
Ditlow, Florence 44, 48, 60, 99

Dives, Josiah 17, 18, 20, 21, 37, 44, 61
Dives, Pomeroy & Stewart (store) 17,
        18, 19, 20, 21, 22, 24, 25, 26,
        27, 28, 29, 32, 33, 34, 36, 37,
        39, 43, 48, 61, 63, 76
Dollar Day 29, 34, 58

E

Easton (store) 101, 102, 104, 115, 135
Eichorn, Pat 44, 48, 57, 64, 96, 108,
        119
Eisenpreis, Alfred 85, 118
Eisenpreis, Bettijane Long 40, 42, 85,
        118
Ellis Mills (store) 78
escalators
   Harrisburg 91
   Reading 54, 83
   Whitner's 77
Executive Training Program 90, 96

F

Federated Department Stores 91
Fowler, Dick & Walker 40, 75, 138
Frew, Ken 44, 64, 92

G

Gimbels 121, 122
Grumbacher, Tim 125, 126, 131,
        141
Grumbacher, Tom 126, 141

H

Hahn Department Stores 45, 99
Harrisburg 18, 19, 21, 25, 26, 28, 29,
        32, 37, 39, 40, 42, 44, 46, 48,
        53, 54, 58, 60, 61, 64, 69, 70,
        73, 91, 97, 101, 102, 107, 108,
        109, 110, 112, 116, 118, 124,
        129, 132, 135, 141
Hayden, Kathy 39, 42
Hazzard, Bettie 58, 70
Hazzard, Russell 48

Heizmann Building (Reading) 21
Hess's 72, 104, 126

I

Isaac Long Store 40, 74, 112

J

Jonas Long's Sons 40, 94

K

Kennedy, John F. 90, 99
Kinsey, Ralph 51, 53
Korczykowski, Barbara 39, 108, 135
Korczykowski, David 114
Kutchever, Anthony 99, 101, 109

L

Lakin, Edwin 79, 81
Lancaster (store) 122, 126
Lazarus (store) 73, 74
Lebanon (store) 99, 101, 104, 119
Levittown Shop-a-Rama 86, 104, 116
Levittown (store) 86, 88, 90, 91, 96, 99,
        104, 111, 115, 116, 124
Levitt, William (builder) 86, 87, 97,
        104
Lit Brothers 90, 107, 114, 116

M

MacWilliam's (Wilkes-Barre) 40
Maday, John 74, 75, 94, 112, 138
Matusek, John 54, 87, 88, 104, 111, 116
Meiser, George M., IX 18, 42, 50, 51,
        62, 77, 83, 120
Midway (store) 105, 111, 118
Miller, Leonard 51, 54, 58, 62, 68, 76,
        83, 99, 102, 107
Mishler, John D. (Globe Store) 18
Mooney, Tom 64, 75, 96, 136, 138
Moyer, Jane 102
Mugford, Dorothy 109
Muhlenberg, Frederick A. (architect)
        24, 94

N

Neshaminy Mall (store) 116

O

Opera House (Harrisburg) 18, 25

P

Penn Mall (proposed) 107, 114, 120
"Pomeroy Day" 57, 58
Pomeroy, Elizabeth 39
Pomeroy, George, Jr. (son) 38, 39, 45, 50
Pomeroy, George S. (founder) 17, 18, 19, 36, 37, 39, 44, 53, 61, 108
Pomeroy, Hollie 19
Pomeroy, Lillie 39
Pomeroy Players 53
Pomeroy's Basement
  Harrisburg 44, 48
  Pottsville 45, 68
  Reading 50, 53, 68, 78, 108, 115
  Wilkes-Barre 111, 136
Potts, Ellen 39, 42
Pottstown (store) 21, 32, 37, 42, 53, 62, 63
Pottsville 21, 33, 37, 42, 44, 46, 53, 54, 58, 61, 64, 70, 72, 85, 110, 118, 119, 135, 141
Public Square (Wilkes-Barre) 40, 64, 73, 74, 94, 109, 111, 112, 124, 136, 138
Puckett, B. Earl 45, 85

R

Raggedy Belsnickel 63
Reading 17, 18, 19, 21, 24, 25, 28, 32, 34, 37, 38, 39, 40, 42, 43, 44, 46, 48, 51, 53, 54, 57, 58, 59, 61, 62, 64, 68, 69, 72, 76, 77, 78, 79, 81, 83, 94, 99, 101, 102, 105, 108, 110, 114, 115, 116, 117, 120, 135, 139, 141, 143
Read's (store) 78

Reed, Stephen (Harrisburg mayor) 119, 130
Ricketts, Ross 42, 50, 59, 108, 112
Rick, John Whitner 77, 78, 109

S

Sachs, Mary 70, 72
Samler, Louis 99, 101
Schuylkill Mall (store) 119
Seivers, James 39, 42, 45, 50, 135
S. Grumbacher & Son (York, Pennsylvania) 99, 124
Shipula, Margaret 57
Smith, Alexander Forbes (Reading architect) 21
Spitalny, Howard 28, 48, 54, 70, 97, 129
Spitalny, Lee 42, 44, 72, 92, 119
Starr, Lee 45, 68, 86, 87, 90, 101, 109, 114, 115
Stewart, John 17, 18, 19, 25, 44, 61
Store Booster 51, 53
Store Chorus 53
store closings
  Downtown Easton 115
  Downtown Harrisburg 129, 132
  Downtown Lebanon 119
  Downtown Pottsville 119
  Downtown Reading 120, 121, 141
  Downtown Wilkes-Barre 124
Strawberry Square (Harrisburg) 70, 118, 119, 129, 130, 131
Strawbridge & Clothier 44, 86, 90, 116
Sullivan, David 78
Syndicate Trading Company 43

T

Tea Rooms
  Harrisburg 46, 48, 97
  Reading 50, 108, 143
Toyland 62, 64
Tropical Storm Agnes 16
  1972 flood 75, 110, 111, 112
Troutman, A.E. Company 90, 119, 120

W

Wanamaker's 53, 68, 75, 86, 90, 107, 112, 116

Watt & Shand 122, 126

"Whiffenpoof Song, The" (Yale University) 38

Whitner, Calvin K. 76

Whitner, C.K. Company 39, 42, 76, 77, 78, 79, 83, 141

Wilkes-Barre 40, 42, 45, 46, 54, 57, 58, 61, 64, 73, 74, 75, 85, 86, 90, 94, 96, 105, 109, 110, 111, 112, 118, 124, 136, 138, 141

William F. Gable Company 34, 36, 39

William Laubach & Sons 101, 102, 104

Willingboro Plaza (New Jersey) 104

Willingboro (store) 104, 124

Witmer, Lois 46, 58, 64, 107, 110, 113, 124, 129, 132

Wyoming Valley Mall (store) 109, 111, 112, 118

ABOUT THE AUTHOR

Michael Lisicky has been credited as a nationally recognized department store "historian," "lecturer," "expert," "guru," "aficionado," "junkie" and "maven" by several major newspapers, such as the *Washington Post*, the *Philadelphia Inquirer*, the *Boston Globe*, the *Pittsburgh Post Gazette*, the *Dallas Morning News*, the *Washington Times*, the *Wilmington New Journal* and the *Baltimore Sun*. He is the author of several best-selling books, including *Wanamaker's: Meet Me at the Eagle*, *Hutzler's: Where Baltimore Shops* and

Author Michael J. Lisicky and Chairman and Chief Executive Officer Albert Boscov, March 2014. *Collection of the author.*

Woodward and Lothrop: A Store Worthy of the Nation's Capital. His book *Gimbels Has It!* was cited as "one of the freshest reads of 2011" by National Public Radio's *Morning Edition* program. Mr. Lisicky has given lecturers at such locations as the New York Public Library, the Boston Public Library, the Historical Society of Pennsylvania, the D.C. Public Library, the 2012 Wanamaker Organ Centennial Week celebration in Philadelphia and at New York Fashion Week. He has also served as a historical consultant for various film, commercial and educational projects. He has been featured in *Fortune* magazine, *Investor's Business Daily* and on National Public Radio and CBS's *Sunday Morning* television program. Mr. Lisicky resides in Baltimore, where he is an oboist with the Baltimore Symphony Orchestra and a master's degree candidate in museum studies at Johns Hopkins University.

Visit us at
www.historypress.net
....
This title is also available as an e-book